GRINDING IT OUT

THE MAKING
OF McDONALD'S

GRINDING IT OUT

THE MAKING
OF McDONALD'S

RAY KROC

WITH ROBERT ANDERSON

CONTEMPORARY
BOOKS, INC.
CHICAGO

Library of Congress Cataloging in Publication Data

Kroc, Ray
    Grinding it out.

    Includes index.
        1. Kroc, Ray.   2. McDonald's Corporation.
    3. Restauranteurs—United States—Biography.
    I. Anderson, Robert, 1930— joint author.   II. Title.
    TX910.5.K76A34   1985   647'.9573   [B]   76-56878
    ISBN 0-8092-5345-3

McDonald's, Big Mac, Filet-O-Fish, Quarter Pounder, Egg McMuffin, Ronald McDonald, and McDonald's All-American High School Band are trademarks owned by McDonald's Corporation.

Journalistic research by Zenona Luc Lopina

Published by Contemporary Books, Inc.
180 North Michigan Avenue, Chicago, Illinois 60601
Manufactured in the United States of America
International Standard Book Number: 0-8092-5345-3

Published simultaneously in Canada by Beaverbooks, Ltd.
195 Allstate Parkway, Valleywood Business Park
Markham, Ontario L3R 4T8 Canada

My wife, Joni, shares with me the enjoyment of dedicating this book to all our friends in the McDonald's family who have helped so greatly in this enterprise.

Preface

"Opportunity is dead in the United States!" "The tax structure has destroyed all incentive!" How often we have heard such laments during the past thirty years, when in fact greater fortunes have been made and higher living standards achieved than ever before on earth!

Those of us who teach courses at graduate schools of business, courses with titles like Entrepreneurship or New Enterprise Management, know that such gloom is unfounded. We have case studies based on true examples of individual success and corporate growth to prove it.

Every now and then a unique and vibrant personality like Ray A. Kroc comes along, a flesh-and-blood example of a Horatio Alger story, who illustrates in practice what one is preaching and who repudiates the lamenters entirely. *Grinding It Out,* Ray Kroc's autobiography and the history of McDonald's Corporation is a dramatic refutation of all who believe that risk takers will no longer be properly rewarded. It reminds us that opportunity abounds, that all one needs is the knack of seizing the chances that exist, of being in the right place at the right time. A little bit of

1

luck helps, yes, but the key element, which too many in our affluent society have forgotten, is still hard work—grinding it out.

Ray Kroc visited our classes at the Amos Tuck School of Business Administration on the Dartmouth College campus in 1974 and returned two years later in March 1976, bringing with him several key members of his corporate team including Fred Turner, McDonald's President and Chief Executive Officer. (The very circumstances of that second visit proved the quality of energy and determination that has marked his business career, for when a major snowstorm closed down the airports in our area, the undaunted Mr. Kroc commandeered a McDonald's bus from his Boston headquarters to drive the stranded executives through the storm.)

With his utter frankness Ray Kroc thoroughly disarmed his audience of sophisticated MBA candidates. On both visits he regaled students with the story of his life and the history of McDonald's, reporting in capsule version all that is spelled out in fuller detail in this autobiography. He fielded all questions that students put to him, exhibiting in his lectures and discussions the qualities which have made him a present-day commercial legend: his tough-minded business philosophy, his virtually compulsive adherence to the fundamental operating strategies designed to attract the family market; his emphasis on such basic qualities as courtesy, cleanliness, and service; and his abiding loyalty to his associates, particularly to those who have served McDonald's since its fledgling years. His talks displayed his humor, competitive zeal, dedication to hard work, and his firm belief that in the United States a person can reach or exceed any reasonable goal. Mr. Kroc is one of the rare individuals who possesses both the charisma of an extraordinary leader who is a great salesman and the passion for detail of an able administrator.

You do not need to hear Ray Kroc speak for long before realizing that *Grinding It Out,* the title he has chosen for his autobiography, is not a humorous reference to the preparation of McDonald's most famous product. Instead, the title brings to mind the long apprenticeship of over thirty years during which Mr. Kroc worked for others as a salesman and sales manager and later in his own small business. For the great opportunity of his life did not come until 1954 when he was fifty-two, an age when some executives are beginning to contemplate the greener pastures of retirement. *Grinding It Out* also appropriately reminds the reader of the staggering investments of time, energy, and capital that were required to develop McDonald's to its current pre-eminence in the fast food service and franchising industries.

This historic year of 1976 will see McDonald's Corporation surpass one billion dollars in total revenue for the first time. Casual students of business history may not realize the significance of the fact that this milestone will be reached during the twenty-second year of the company's history.   To put this accomplishment in some perspective, the reader should be reminded that IBM, highly renowned as a growth company, did not achieve the one-billion-dollar sales mark until its forty-sixth year, 1957. And Xerox, another corporation famous for its growth, took sixty-three years before making the billion-dollar club in 1969. Polaroid has yet to attain annual sales of a billion dollars although the corporation was founded in 1937.   Despite the changes in price levels since Xerox Corporation was founded in 1906, these statistics on sales or total revenue do provide some sense of proportion to the corporate history of McDonald's and its unprecedented growth.

Though the business history of McDonald's is fascinating in and of itself, it is only one facet of *Grinding It Out*. For the practices pioneered or perfected by McDonald's under Ray Kroc's leadership have revolutionized an entire food service industry, changed eating habits throughout the world and raised customer expectations. Who among us is not now less tolerant of slow service, overpriced meals, soggy french fries, or a lack of cleanliness in eating places?

Mr. Kroc's book is not only a fascinating memoir, it is a welcome addition to the literature available to students of business in general. *Grinding It Out* will be uniquely valuable to those who aspire to build their own enterprise, whether the potential founder is in his or her late teens, early fifties, or at any age in between.

Paul D. Paganucci
Associate Dean and Professor
   of Business Administration
Amos Tuck School of Business Administration
Dartmouth College

Hanover, New Hampshire
June 29, 1976

1

There is a tide in the affairs of men,
Which, taken at the flood, leads on to fortune;
Omitted, all the voyage of their life
Is bound in shallows and in miseries.
On such a full sea are we now afloat,
And we must take the current when it serves,
Or lose our ventures.

—Shakespeare, *Julius Caesar*

I have always believed that each man makes his own happiness and is responsible for his own problems. It is a simple philosophy. I think it must have been passed along to me in the peasant bones of my Bohemian ancestors. But I like it because it works, and I find that it functions as well for me now that I am a multimillionaire as it did when I was selling paper cups for thirty-five dollars a week and playing the piano part-time to support my wife and baby daughter back in the early twenties. It follows, obviously, that a man must take advantage of any opportunity that comes along, and I have always done that, too. After seventeen years of selling paper cups for Lily Tulip Cup Company and climbing to the top of the organization's sales ladder, I saw opportunity appear in the form of an ugly, six-spindled milk-shake machine called a Multimixer, and I grabbed it. It wasn't easy to give up security and a well-paying job to strike out on my own. My wife was shocked and incredulous. But my success soon calmed her

5

fears, and I plunged gleefully into my campaign to sell a Multimixer to every drug store soda fountain and dairy bar in the nation. It was a rewarding struggle. I loved it. Yet I was alert to other opportunities. I have a saying that goes, "As long as you're green you're growing, as soon as you're ripe you start to rot." And I was as green as a Shamrock Shake on St. Patrick's Day when I heard about an incredible thing that was happening with my Multimixer out in California.

The vibrations came in calls from voluntary prospects in different parts of the country. One day it would be a restaurant owner in Portland, Oregon; the next day a soda fountain operator in Yuma, Arizona; the following week, a dairy-bar manager in Washington, D.C. In essence, the message was always the same, "I want one of those mixers of yours like the McDonald brothers have in San Bernardino, California." I got curiouser and curiouser. Who were these McDonald brothers, and why were customers picking up on the Multimixer from them when I had similar machines in lots of places? (The machine, by this time had five spindles instead of six.) So I did some checking and was astonished to learn that the McDonalds had not one Multimixer, not two or three, but eight! The mental picture of eight Multimixers churning out forty shakes at one time was just too much to be believed. These mixers sold at $150 apiece, mind you, and that was back in 1954. The fact that this was taking place in San Bernardino, which was a quiet town in those days, practically in the desert, made it all the more amazing.

I flew out to Los Angeles one day and made some routine calls with my representative there. Then, bright and early the next morning, I drove the sixty miles east to San Bernardino. I cruised past the McDonald's location about 10 A.M., and I was not terrifically impressed. There was a smallish octagonal building, a very humble sort of structure situated on a corner lot about 200 feet square. It was a typical, ordinary-looking drive-in. As the 11 o'clock opening time approached, I parked my car and watched the helpers begin to show up—all men, dressed in spiffy white shirts and trousers and white paper hats. I liked that. They began to move supplies from a long, low shed at the back of the property. They trundled four-wheeled carts loaded with sacks of potatoes, cartons of meat, cases of milk and soft drinks, and boxes of buns into the octagonal building. Something was definitely happening here, I told myself. The tempo of their work picked up until they were bustling around like ants at a picnic. Then the cars began to arrive, and the lines started to form. Soon the parking lot was full and people were marching up to the windows and back to their cars with bags full of hamburgers. Eight Multimixers churning away at one time began to seem a lot less farfetched in light of this steady procession of customers lockstepping up to the windows. Slightly dazed but still somewhat dubious, I got out of my car and took a place in line.

"Say, what's the attraction here?" I asked a swarthy man in a seersucker suit who was just in front of me.

"Never eaten here before?" he asked.

"Nope."

"Well, you'll see," he promised. "You'll get the best hamburger you ever ate for fifteen cents. And you don't have to wait and mess around tipping waitresses."

I left the line and walked around behind the building, where several men were hunkered down in the shade baseball-catcher style, resting their backs against the wall and gnawing away on hamburgers. One wore a carpenter's apron; he must have walked over from a nearby construction site. He looked up at me with an open, friendly gaze; so I asked him how often he came there for lunch.

"Every damned day," he said without a pause in his chewing. "It sure beats the old lady's cold meatloaf sandwiches."

It was a hot day, but I noticed that there were no flies swarming around the place. The men in the white suits were keeping everything neat and clean as they worked. That impressed the hell out of me, because I've always been impatient with poor housekeeping, especially in restaurants. I observed that even the parking lot was being kept free of litter.

In a bright yellow convertible sat a strawberry blond who looked like she had lost her way to the Brown Derby or the Paramount cafeteria. She was demolishing a hamburger and a bag of fries with a demure precision that was fascinating. Emboldened by curiosity, I approached her and said I was taking a traffic survey.

"If you don't mind telling me, how often do you come here?" I asked.

"Anytime I am in the neighborhood," she smiled. "And that's as often as possible, because my boyfriend lives here."

Whether she was teasing or being candid or simply using the mention of her boyfriend as a ploy to discourage this inquisitive middle-aged guy who might be a masher, I couldn't tell, and I cared not at all. It was not her sex appeal but the obvious relish with which she devoured the hamburger that made my pulse begin to hammer with excitement. Her appetite was magnified for me by the many people in cars that filled the parking lot, and I could feel myself getting wound up like a pitcher with a no-hitter going. This had to be the most amazing merchandising operation I had ever seen!

I don't remember whether I ate a hamburger for lunch that day or not. I went back to my car and waited around until about 2:30 in the afternoon, when the crowd dwindled down to just an occasional customer. Then I went over to the building and introduced myself to Mac and Dick McDonald. They were delighted to see me ("Mr. Multimixer" they called me), and I warmed up to them immediately. We made a date to get together for dinner that evening so they could tell me all about their operation.

I was fascinated by the simplicity and effectiveness of the system they described that night. Each step in producing the limited menu was stripped down to its essence and accomplished with a minimum of effort. They sold hamburgers and cheeseburgers only. The burgers were a tenth of a pound of meat, all fried the same way, for fifteen cents. You got a slice of cheese on it for four cents more. Soft drinks were ten cents, sixteen-ounce milk shakes were twenty cents, and coffee was a nickel.

After dinner, the brothers took me over to visit their architect, who was just completing work on the design of a new drive-in building for them. It was neat. The building was red and white with touches of yellow, and had snazzy looking oversized windows. It had some improved serving area features over those being used in the McDonald's octagonal structure. And it had washrooms in back. In the existing building, customers had to walk to the back of the lot to the long, low building that was a combination warehouse, office, and washrooms. What made the new building unique was a set of arches that went right through the roof. There was a tall sign out front with arches that had neon tubes lighting the underside. I could see plenty of problems there. The arches of the sign looked like they would topple over in a strong wind, and those neon lights would need constant attention to keep them from fading out and looking tacky. But I liked the basic idea of the arches and most of the other features of the design, too.

That night in my motel room I did a lot of heavy thinking about what I'd seen during the day. Visions of McDonald's restaurants dotting crossroads all over the country paraded through my brain. In each store, of course, were eight Multimixers whirring away and paddling a steady flow of cash into my pockets.

The next morning I got up with a plan of action in mind. I was on the scene when McDonald's windows opened for business. What followed was pretty much a repeat of the scenario that had played the previous day, but I watched it with undiminished fascination. I observed some things a lot more closely, though, and with more awareness, thanks to my conversation with the McDonald brothers. I noted how the griddleman handled his job; how he slapped the patties of meat down when he turned them, and how he kept the sizzling griddle surface scraped. But I paid particular attention to the french-fry operation. The brothers had indicated this was one of the key elements in their sales success, and they'd described the process. But I had to see for myself how it worked. There had to be a secret something to make french fries that good.

Now, to most people, a french-fried potato is a pretty uninspiring object. It's fodder, something to kill time chewing between bites of hamburger and swallows of milk shake. That's your ordinary french fry. The McDonald's french fry was in an entirely different league. They lavished attention on it. I didn't know it then, but one day I would, too. The french fry would become almost sacrosanct for me, its preparation a ritual to be followed religiously. The McDonald brothers kept their potatoes—top quality Idaho spuds, about eight ounces apiece—piled in bins in their back warehouse building. Since rats and mice and other varmints like to eat potatoes, the walls of the bins were of two layers of small-mesh chicken wire. This kept the critters out and allowed fresh air to circulate among the potatoes. I watched the spuds being bagged up and followed their trip by four-wheeled cart to the octagonal drive-in building. There they were carefully peeled, leaving a tiny proportion of skin on, and then they were cut into long sections and dumped into large sinks of cold water. The french-fry man, with his sleeves rolled up to the shoulders, would plunge his arms into the floating schools of potatoes and gently stir them. I could see the water turning white with starch. This was drained off and the residual starch was rinsed from the glistening morsels with a flexible spray hose. Then the potatoes went into wire baskets, stacked in production-line fashion next to the deep-fry vats. A common problem with french fries is that they're fried in oil that has been used for chicken or for some other cooking. Any restaurant will deny it, but almost all of them do it. A very small scandal, perhaps, but a scandal nonetheless, and it's just one of the little crimes that have given the french fry a bad name while ruining the appetites of countless Americans. There was no adulteration of the oil for cooking french fries by the McDonald brothers. Of course, they weren't tempted. They had nothing else to cook in it. Their potatoes sold at ten cents for a three-ounce bag, and let me tell you, that was a rare bargain. The customers knew it, too. They bought prodigious quantities of those potatoes. A big aluminum salt shaker was attached to a long chain by the french-fry window, and it was kept going like a Salvation Army girl's tambourine.

The McDonald's approach to french fries was a very interesting process to me and, I was happy to observe, it was every bit as simple as the McDonald boys had told me it was. I was convinced that I had it down pat in my head, and that anybody could do it if he followed those individual steps to the letter. That was just one of the many mistakes I would make in my dealings with the McDonald brothers.

After the lunch-hour rush had abated, I got together with Mac and Dick McDonald again. My enthusiasm for their operation was genuine, and I hoped it would be infectious and rally them in favor of the plan I had mapped out in my mind.

"I've been in the kitchens of a lot of restaurants and drive-ins selling Multimixers around the country," I told them, "and I have never seen anything to equal the potential of this place of yours. Why don't you open a series of units like this? It would be a gold mine for you and for me, too, because every one would boost my Multimixer sales. What d'you say?"

Silence.

I felt like I'd dragged my tie in my soup or something. The two brothers just sat there looking at me. Then Mac gave that little wince that sometimes passes for a smile in New England and turned around in his chair to point up at the hill overlooking the restaurant.

"See that big white house with the wide front porch?" he asked. "That's our home and we love it. We sit out on the porch in the evenings and watch the sunset and look down on our place here. It's peaceful. We don't need any more problems than we have in keeping this place going. More places, more problems. We are in a position to enjoy life now, and that's just what we intend to do."

His approach was utterly foreign to my thinking, so it took me a few minutes to reorganize my arguments. But it soon became apparent that further discussion along that line would be futile, so I said they could have their cake and eat it too by getting somebody else to open the other places for them. I could still peddle my Multimixers in the chain.

"It'll be a lot of trouble," Dick McDonald objected. "Who could we get to open them for us?"

I sat there feeling a sense of certitude begin to envelope me. Then I leaned forward and said, "Well, what about me?"

2

When I flew back to Chicago that fateful day in 1954, I had a freshly signed contract with the McDonald brothers in my brief-case. I was a battle-scarred veteran of the business wars, but I was still eager to go into action. I was 52 years old. I had diabetes and incipient arthritis. I had lost my gall bladder and most of my thyroid gland in earlier campaigns. But I was convinced that the best was ahead of me. I was still green and growing, and I was flying along at an altitude slightly higher than the plane. It was bright and sunny up there above the clouds. You could see nothing but clear skies and endless acres of billowy hummocks all the way from the Colorado River to Lake Michigan. But everything turned gray and threatening as we began our descent into Chicago. Perhaps I should have taken that as an omen.

My thoughts, however, as we glided through the churning blackness, were on those hidden streets and alleys below where I had grown up along with the century.

I was born in Oak Park, just west of Chicago's city limits, in 1902. My father, Louis Kroc, was a Western Union man. He had gone to work for the company when he was twelve years old and slowly but steadily worked his way up. He had left school in the eighth grade, and he was determined that I would finish high school. I was the wrong kid for that. My brother, Bob, who was born three and a half years after me, and my sister, Lorraine, who came along five years after him, were much more inclined to studies. In fact, Bob became a professor, a medical researcher, and we had almost nothing in common, he and I. For many years we found it difficult even to talk to each other.

My mother, Rose, was a loving soul. She ran a neat, well-organized house. But she did not carry cleanliness to the extremes her mother did. I will never forget my grandmother's kitchen. The floor was covered with newspapers all week long. Then, on Saturday, the newspapers would be taken up and the floor—which was already as clean as a nun's cowl—would be scrubbed vigorously with steaming hot soapy water. After it was rinsed and dried, back down would go a fresh covering of newspapers to protect it in the week ahead. That was the old way Grandma had brought from Bohemia, and she was not about to change. My mother gave piano lessons to bring in extra money, and she expected me to help with the housework. I didn't mind. In fact, I prided myself on being able to sweep and clean and make beds as well as anyone.

Children were to be seen but not heard in adult company in those days, but I never felt left out. For example, my father belonged to a singing group that often met in our house. My brother and I had to stay upstairs and amuse ourselves while my mother played the piano and the men sang. As soon as the music stopped below, Bob and I would drop whatever game we were playing and rush back to the sewing room, which was right above the kitchen. I would pull the warm-air grate out of the floor (that was before we had central heating, and floor registers were used to let heated air rise to the upper rooms). My mother would put a dish of whatever refreshments she was serving on a tray that my father had affixed to an old broom handle, then she would hoist it up to us. It was a delightful feeling of adventure, because my mother pretended to be sneaking the food away without letting the other adults know.

I was never much of a reader when I was a boy. Books bored

me. I liked action. But I spent a lot of time thinking about things. I'd imagine all kinds of situations and how I would handle them.

"What are you doing Raymond?" my mother would ask.

"Nothing. Just thinking."

"Daydreaming you mean," she'd say. "Danny Dreamer is at it again."

They called me Danny Dreamer a lot, even later when I was in high school and would come home all excited about some scheme I'd thought up. I never considered my dreams wasted energy; they were invariably linked to some form of action. When I dreamed about having a lemonade stand, for example, it wasn't long before I set up a lemonade stand. I worked hard at it, and I sold a lot of lemonade. I worked at a grocery store one summer when I was still in grammar school. I worked at my uncle's drug store. I worked in a tiny music store I'd started with two friends. I worked at something whenever possible. Work is the meat in the hamburger of life. There is an old saying that *all work and no play makes Jack a dull boy.* I never believed it because, for me, work was play. I got as much pleasure out of it as I did from playing baseball.

Baseball was truly the national pastime in those days, of course, and our neighborhood games in the alley behind my house were grand contests. My father was a baseball buff, too, and he began taking me to see the Chicago Cubs play in the old west side ballpark when I was seven years old. I saw plenty of double plays pulled off by the Cubs' famous Tinker to Evers to Chance combination. The Cubs were contenders then, and I knew all the statistics about every player down to his shoe size. My father belonged to the same lodge as Joe Tinker, and that gave me the upper hand over other kids in our frequent arguments about baseball players, especially when it came to the Cubs. I had to know more about it, of course, because my old man knew Joe Tinker personally. What sweet strife those alley altercations were. And how fiercely we played the game—with a garbage can lid for home base, a well-chewed bat (pocked from hitting stones for batting practice), and a ball bandaged in black friction tape. How agonizing it was though when my mother would step out onto the back porch and call, "Raymond! It's time to come in and practice." The other guys would mimic her voice and inflection jeeringly as the chesty expert on the Cubs shouted resentfully, "I'm coming!" and shuffled off to submit to his mother's piano instructions.

I took to the piano naturally.   My facility at the keyboard pleased my mother, and I'm still thankful to her for those hours of disciplined practice, although at the time I often thought her demands were excessive. I became proficient enough to acquire a minor reputation in the neighborhood and to prompt the choirmaster of the Harvard Congregational Church to recruit me to play the organ for his practice sessions—a slight lapse of judgment on his part. I was willing and able, but the stately chords of the hymns began to oppress me. I fidgeted on the bench of the old pump organ through the entire second half of the evening. How those people managed to put up with all the interruptions, the lecturing of the choirmaster, and his repetition of the same passages over and over again I could not understand. Moreover, the music itself was so saccharine and slow that I was suffocating up there in the organ loft. When he concluded the last hymn of that seemingly interminable session and said, "That's it, ladies and gentlemen, good night." I reacted spontaneously by playing the old vaudeville tune tag, "Shave and a haircut, two-bits." Naturally, the choirmaster was scandalized.   He never reprimanded me for that little breach of decorum, but he never asked me to play the organ again either.

My musical interest was more commercial. I admired the piano players in the big Woolworth and Kresge stores in Chicago's Loop. They would play and sing to attract customers into the music department, where there were racks of sheet music and accessories for sale. If you saw a piece of music that interested you and wanted to hear the arrangement, the piano man would oblige with a snappy rendition. I daydreamed that I was a piano man too, and the opportunity came the summer after I started high school.

I had spent the previous summer and lunch hours during the school year working in my uncle Earl Edmund Sweet's drug store soda fountain in Oak Park. That was where I learned that you could influence people with a smile and enthusiasm and sell them a sundae when what they'd come for was a cup of coffee. In any event, I saved just about every penny I earned and finally had enough in the bank to go into the music store business with two friends. We each invested a hundred dollars and rented a little hole-in-the-wall shop for twenty-five dollars a month. We sold sheet music and novelty instruments such as ocarinas, harmonicas, and ukuleles. I was the piano man, and I did a lot of playing and singing but not much selling. The sad truth is that we didn't do enough business to put in your eye. We had a month-to-month lease, and after a few months we gave it up, sold our stock of goods to another music store, divided the money that was left three ways, and that was that.

My sophomore year in high school passed like a funeral. I began to feel about school the way I had felt earlier about the Boy Scouts. It was simply too slow for me. I'd been eager to become a Boy Scout, and I enjoyed it for a while. They made me the bugler. But a bugle is a very limited instrument, and I found myself doing the same things over and over in meetings. It was small potatoes. I wasn't progressing, so I said to hell with it. School was the same—full of aggravations and little progress.

The only thing I really enjoyed about school was debating. Here was an activity I could get my teeth into—figuratively, of course—but I would not have hesitated to bite a debate opponent if it would have advanced my argument. I loved being the center of attention, persuading the audience that my side was right. One debate that I remember in particular was on the question "Should Smoking Be Abolished?" As happened more often than not, I was on the side of the underdogs, trying to defend smoking. It was a very spirited exchange, but my opponents made the mistake of painting the demon tobacco too black, too vile, too evil to be countenanced by a sane society. Rhetoric is fine as long as it maintains some contact with reality. So I attacked their excesses by telling very simply the story of my great-grandfather and his beloved pipe. Grandpa Phossie, we called him, which means Grandpa Beard. I told of the hardships he'd undergone in Bohemia and how he had made his way to the United States. I related in pithy detail how he had built a home for his family with the sweat of his brow. Now he had little time left in life and few pleasures beyond throwing a stick for his little dog to fetch and looking into the swirls of smoke from his ancient pipe to recall scenes from happier days. "Who among you," I asked, "would deprive that whitebearded old man of one of his last comforts on earth, his beloved pipe?" I was delighted to note that there were tears in the eyes of some of the girls in the auditorium as I finished. I wished my father could have heard that applause. It might have made up for some of his disappointment in my lack of scholastic interest.

As school ended that spring, the United States entered World War I. I took a job selling coffee beans and novelties door-to-door. I was confident I could make my way in the world and saw no reason to return to school. Besides, the war effort was more important. Everyone was singing "Over There." And that's where I wanted to be. My parents objected strenuously, but I finally talked them into letting me join up as a Red Cross ambulance driver. I had to lie about my age, of course, but even my grandmother could accept that. In my company, which assembled in Connecticut for training, was another fellow who had lied about his age to get in. He was regarded as a strange duck, because vhenever we had time off and went out on the town to chase girls, he stayed in camp drawing pictures. His name was Walt Disney.

The Armistice was signed just before I was to get on the boat to ship out to France. So I went marching back home to Chicago, wondering what to do next. My parents talked me into trying school again, but I lasted only one semester. Algebra had not improved in my absence.

I wanted to be out selling and playing the piano for money, and that's what I did. I got a territory selling ribbon novelties, and I took to it like a duck takes to water. I'd have a sample room set up in whatever hotel I was staying in, and I'd learn what each buyer's taste was and sell to it. No self-respecting pitcher throws the same way to every batter, and no self-respecting salesman makes the same pitch to every client. In 1919 anyone making twenty-five or thirty dollars a week was doing well, and it wasn't long before—on good weeks with a lot of musical jobs—I was making more money than my father.

I was a regular "sheik" at seventeen—cocky and probably

annoying to be around. Rudolph Valentino was driving the girls wild then, and I modeled myself after him. I parted my rather wiry hair in the middle and plastered pomade on it to get that slicked-back, patent-leather look. I bought sharp clothes and smoked Melachrino cork-tipped Turkish cigarettes when I went out on dates. After my date and I were seated I would produce my box of imported cigarettes with a flair and place it on the table to show how sophisticated I was. This was just a passing phase, but it still embarrasses me to recall it, because there's nothing I dislike more than phony sophistication. In fact, I take a kind of perverse pleasure in the memory of the night most of the "sheik" was shocked out of me.

A musician named Herbie Mintz, who always knew where work was to be found, confided to me that he knew a nightclub that was looking for a piano player with my kind of style. It was located way down in Calumet City, but it paid well above the going rates. I jumped at it. Getting from Oak Park on the west side to the far southeast suburb was a major undertaking. I rode several different buses and trains, but somehow I made it on time for the 9 P.M. opening.

The place turned out to be a bordello. The downstairs "cabaret" where we played was decorated in the most god-awful, garish gay-nineties plush and gilt you could imagine. It was presided over by a madame who must have weighed 200 pounds. I have never seen such a getup as she wore. Her hair and makeup were as flamboyant as the decor of the place, and she reeked of cheap perfume. I got plenty of good whiffs of it as she hung over me and sang to my accompaniment. I can still see her yellow pearls bouncing on that heaving bosom, those rings flashing on her pudgy fingers, as she belted out songs in her gravelly voice.

Between sets, when she got a lull in directing traffic to the bedrooms upstairs, Big Momma came over to the piano and warmed up to me.

"Where do you live, honey?" she asked.

I had all I could do to keep my voice from quavering as I told her I came from Oak Park.

"Well, now, that's too far for you to travel late at night. Tonight, you stay here."

I was afraid to say no, and I squirmed uneasily on the piano bench the rest of the evening, watching her out of the corner of my eye and hoping she'd keep her distance. The customers were a pretty hard and rowdy lot, so I had no reassurance there. Just before the final set, I sidled over to the bartender and called him aside. I strove mightily to act casual and keep my voice steady.

"Listen, we have only one more set to play and I've got a long ride home. I don't want to hang around," I said. "So how about paying me off right now?"

Without a word, poker-faced but knowing, he reached under the bar and handed me my money. I hurried over to the men's room, where I stuffed the cash into my sock. I didn't trust anybody in that place. After the set, while the other guys in the band were still putting away their instruments, I was running down the street, putting as much distance as possible between me and that 200-pound madame.

I never went back.

My selling job with the ribbon novelty outfit began to hit its limits before long. It was interesting, but I could see that I was not cut out for a career of peddling rosebuds for farm wives to sew on garters and bedcushions. So I gave it up in the summer of 1919 and got a job playing in a band at Paw-Paw Lake, Michigan. That was a genuine taste of the era. We were really "with-it," in our striped blazers and straw boaters. Talk about your "flaming youth" and "Charleston-crazed kids," wow.

I played in a dime-a-dance pavilion called the Edgewater. The lake was a very popular summer resort in those days, and we used to draw people from the hotels all around. Late in the afternoon our whole band would get aboard one of the ferry boats that plied the lake, and we would steam along the shoreline playing frantically. One of our boys would get up in the bow with a megaphone and call out, "Dancing tonight at the Edgewater, don't miss out on the fun!"

Among the regular crowd at the lake were two sisters named Ethel and Maybelle Fleming. They came from Melrose Park, Illinois, and they helped during the summer at a hotel their parents owned directly across the lake from the Edgewater. Their father was an engineer in Chicago and was an infrequent visitor at the lake. Their mother ran the hotel, did all the cooking, and much of the housekeeping. She was a remarkably energetic woman. The sisters would canoe over to the pavilion in the evenings and hang around with our crowd. After the dancing was finished, we'd all go out for hamburgers or have wiener roasts or go canoeing in the moonlight.

Ethel and I were an item in the group almost from the start. By the time the summer was over, we were getting very interested in each other.

My next job was in Chicago's financial district as a board marker on the New York Curb, as the market that became the American Stock Exchange used to be called. My employer was a firm named Wooster-Thomas. A very substantial sound to that, I thought. My job was to read the ticker tape and translate the symbols from it into prices that I posted on the blackboard for the scrutiny of the gentlemen who frequented our office. I later learned that the impressive-sounding name fronted a bucket-shop operation that was selling watered stock all over the place.

Early in 1920, my father was promoted to a management position in ADT, a subsidiary of Western Union, and was transferred to New York. I was very reluctant to leave Ethel; we were talking about getting married as soon as possible, but my mother insisted that I move east with them. I was able to get a job with the Wooster-Thomas office in New York. This was in the cashier's cage, however, and I didn't like it nearly as well as the more active work of marking up boards. As it turned out, I didn't have to worry about it much more than a year. One day when I went to work, the office was boarded up, and the sheriff had posted a notice that they'd gone bankrupt. That hurt! They owed me a week's pay plus vacation time. I had been planning to take my time off the following week and go to Chicago to visit Ethel. Now I could see no reason for waiting, so I left the next day. My mother was upset when I told her I was leaving and that I didn't want to come back, but there wasn't much she could do about it. She hated New York herself. After I left she worked on my father until he finally gave up his promotion and moved back to Chicago.

In 1922, Ethel and I decided we'd waited long enough. I was still a minor, but I was going to be married come hell or high water. When I told my father about it, he got an adamant glint in his eye and said, "Impossible!"

"Sir?"

"I said, Raymond, that it is not possible for you to get married. You must first have a steady job. And I don't mean working as an errand boy or a bellhop in a hotel. I mean something substantial."

A few days later I went to work selling Lily brand paper cups. I don't know what appealed to me so much about paper cups. Perhaps it was mostly because they were so innovative and upbeat. But I sensed from the outset that paper cups were part of the way America was headed. I guess my father must have agreed. At least he raised no further objections, and Ethel and I were married.

3

A phenomenon of the early twenties that has passed into the folklore of great American frauds was the sale of underwater real estate in Florida. The men who sold those lots were made out to be the slickest con artists in the country. The stories of how they took gullible tourists into the swamps and separated them from their money in exchange for deeds to property that only an alligator could love made lively reading in New York and Chicago newspapers. But the whole business was blown way out of proportion, and many honest salesmen were maligned in the process. I ought to know, because I was one of the best of them.

I went to Florida because the paper cup business was a bear—it went into hibernation in the winter—and a salesman had to live off whatever layers of fat he'd managed to build up in the summer. Of course, in those first years, that wasn't much for me. Paper cups were not an easy sale when I hit the streets with my Lily Cup·sample case in 1922. The immigrant restaurant owners I approached with my sales pitch shook their heads and said, "Naw, I hev glasses, dey costs me chipper." My main sales were to soda fountains. Washing glasses was a real pain in the elbow for

23

them. If they had water hot enough to sterilize the glasses, it would create a cloud of steam coming out of their soda fountain. Paper cups got around that problem. They were more hygienic, and they eliminated breakage and losses through unreturned takeout orders. Those elements became the principal points in my sales story. I was green as grass, but I sensed that the potential for paper cups was great and that I would do well if I could overcome the inertia of tradition. It wasn't easy. I pounded the pavement in my territory from early morning until 5:00 or 5:30 in the afternoon. I would have worked longer, I suppose, but I had another job waiting for me at 6 o'clock—playing piano at radio station WGES in Oak Park. The studio was in the Oak Park Arms Hotel, just a couple of blocks away from the building where Ethel and I had moved into a second-floor flat.

I teamed up with Harry Sosnik, the regular staff pianist, and we became known as "The Piano Twins" to listeners who tuned in to hear us through their earphones. We were gaining in popularity, with our pictures beginning to appear on the covers of sheet music, when Harry left to become the pianist with the well-known Zez Confrey orchestra. He was featured in a highly successful Confrey composition "Kitten on the Keys." Later Harry formed his own orchestra and did well; he became a fixture on the Hit Parade show on radio. I was promoted to staff pianist at WGES, and this made my double workday complete. I had to arrive at the station promptly at 6 P.M. and play for two hours. I was off from 8 to 10 P.M., and then I returned to work until 2 o'clock in the morning. A few hours later—7 or 7:15 A.M.—I'd be off with my sample case in pursuit of paper cup orders. The only break in this routine was on Sunday, my day off from Lily Cup. But we had afternoon hours at the radio station then. There was no programming on Monday nights—silent nights, they were called. But on Mondays I usually played theater dates with Hugh Marshall, our announcer. Sometimes in the winter months I would be held up by traffic, and I'd arrive at the station a couple of minutes late to find Hugh Marshall stalling for time by chattering brightly into the microphone as he glowered and shook his fist at me. I'd slip out of my coat and muffler and, still wearing my galoshes, launch into some preliminary rambling on the piano, sight reading the music.

Sometimes a female vocalist I'd never seen before would be there, and I'd have to accompany her on songs I'd never heard, much less practiced. Often I knew nothing about the singer, her timing or style, and I'd have to fake and flounder. But it usually came out pretty well. At newsbreak, I would run to the washroom, kick off my galoshes, splash some cold water on my face, and wash my hands. That spruced me up enough to play with gusto until 8 o'clock, when I could hurry home to dinner and relax for an hour or so. The second shift, from ten at night until two in the morning, was usually a lively session. I enjoyed it, but I was beginning to run out of gas by the time we went off the air. When I reached home, I would start undressing as I climbed up the stairs, and I'd already be asleep when my head hit the pillow.

One of my incidental tasks at the radio station was to hire talent to build up the programs. One evening a couple of fellows who called themselves Sam and Henry came in to audition. They gave me their routine, a few songs and vaudevillian patter. Their singing was lousy but the jokes weren't too bad, so I hired them for five dollars apiece. They kept working on their characters and developed a southern Negro dialogue that was a huge success. That team went on to make show business history, later changing the name of their act to Amos and Andy. Another pair of entertainers I worked with at WGES, also hired for a pittance, were Little Jack Little and Tommy Malie. Jack's distinctive piano style caught on, and he formed a popular dance band. Tommy, who really had a way with a song, composed danceable tunes with tender lyrics. He wrote, among others, "Jealous" and "Looking at the World Through Rose-Colored Glasses." There was something especially poignant in those songs coming from Tommy, because he was born with both arms stunted, ending at the elbows. The royalties from his music would have allowed him to live in comfort for life, but Tommy ended up a penniless alcoholic.

Ethel used to complain once in a while about the amount of time I spent away from home working. Looking back on it now, I guess it was kind of unfair. But I was driven by ambition. I hated to be idle for a minute. I was determined to live well and have nice things, too, and we could do so with the income from my two jobs. I used to comb through the advertisements in the local newspaper for notices of house sales in the wealthier suburbs—River Forest, Hinsdale, and Wheaton. I haunted these sales and picked up pieces of elegant furniture at bargain basement prices.

Eventually, I was able to get Saturday nights off at the radio station, and this became the big night of the week for Ethel and me. I had to work half a day Saturday at the Lily Cup office in the Loop, and they would pass out the paychecks as we left. I'd stop at the bank on my way home and cash my check, putting most of it in savings and keeping enough for the week's groceries and incidental expenses. Then Ethel would fix an early supper. Later we would put on our best clothes and take the elevated into Chicago to see whatever shows were playing—the "Ziegfeld Follies," "George White's Scandals," and many legitimate plays; we saw them all from our dollar seats up in havenot heaven. After the show we would go to Henrici's for coffee and pick up the Sunday papers on our way home.

Those were the good old days in many ways. A lot of financiers and business moguls seemed to be looking at the world through the rose-colored glasses that Tommy Malie sang about, and if great men like Secretary of Commerce Herbert Hoover believed we had reached the point of perpetual prosperity, who was to disagree? My cup sales kept growing as I learned how to plan my work and work my plan. My confidence grew at the same rate. I found that my customers appreciated a straightforward approach. They would buy if I made my pitch and asked for their order without a lot of beating around the bush. Too many salesmen, I found, would make a good presentation and convince the client, but they couldn't recognize that critical moment when they should have stopped talking. If I ever noticed my prospect starting to fidget, glancing at his watch or looking out the window or shuffling the papers on his desk, I would stop talking right then and ask for his order. In the summertime when the Cubs were in town, I planned my work so I would arrive at the ball park just before game time. I sold paper cups to a brash youngster named Bill Veeck, who ran concessions in the park for his father. I liked him, but I was afraid that his impertinence would get him in a lot of trouble. Over the years, I've never seen any reason to alter that assessment. Bill was a go-getter, but more than once I found him sleeping on a bag of peanuts. I'd tell him he was supposed to be out selling those things, not using them for a mattress. Baseball was a much faster game in those days. I could sun myself in a bleacher seat for nine innings and still get in a couple of hours of selling after the game. Nowadays you're lucky if the game is finished before sundown. And they played great baseball back there in the twenties, too. Of course, Roger Kahn was right when he said in *The Boys of Summer* that "... baseball skill relates inversely to age. The older a man gets, the better a ball player he was when he was young, according to the watery eye of memory." And the same holds true for the ball players one watched with the zestful involvement of youth. I can still picture Hack Wilson's stance at the plate, and the sight of Babe Ruth calling that home run off Charley Root in Wrigley Field. I drove to the park for that game in my old Model A Ford to get in line for tickets at two o'clock in the morning. It was cold as hell, and guys had built fires in the gutter and were swigging gin to keep warm. I declined at first when they passed the bottle around, but I finally had a belt or two. After daybreak it warmed up, but those fellows kept hitting that gin. I saw them later during the game. I looked down between the bleacher seats and there they were sprawled on the ground dead drunk; I guess they never saw a single play. When I mention Ruth calling his home run, I saw the motion, but I don't think he really called it. That was all in the minds of the sports-writers.

My daughter, Marilyn, was born in October 1924, and having this additional responsibility made me work even harder. That winter was a particularly tough one for the paper cup business. Everything slowed down except for the hospital and medical clinic sales, and I didn't have any of those places for customers. I didn't do very well, because I thought of the customer first. I didn't try to force an order on a soda fountain operator when I could see that his business had fallen off because of cold weather and he didn't need the damn cups. My philosophy was one of helping my customer, and if I couldn't sell him by helping him improve his own sales, I felt I wasn't doing my job. I collected my salary of thirty-five dollars a week just the same. But my company was losing money on me by paying it, and I hated that. I vowed that I wouldn't allow it to happen again the next winter.

In the spring of 1925 I began to hit my stride as a salesman.

There was a German restaurant called Walter Powers on the south side of Chicago. The manager was a Prussian martinet named Bittner. He always listened politely to my sales pitch, but he always, just as politely, said "Nein, danke," and dismissed me. One day when I called on the place I saw a gleaming Marmon automobile parked at the rear entrance. I was looking it over admiringly when a man came out of the restaurant and approached me.

"Do you like that car?" he asked.

"Yes sir!" I replied. "Say, you're Mr. Powers, aren't you?"

He said he was and I told him, "Mr. Powers, if I could aspire to own a car like this, you could have the Rock Island and heaven, too."

We chatted for some time about automobiles. I told him that I had ridden in the rumble seat on the outside of a Stutz Bearcat, and he agreed that had to be one of life's finer experiences. After thirty minutes or so of shooting the breeze, he asked me who I represented and I told him.

"Are we giving you any business?" he asked. I shook my head and he added, "Well, you hang in there and keep trying. Herr Bittner's a hard man, but he's fair and square, and if you deserve it he'll give you a chance."

A few weeks later, I got my first order from Bittner, and it was a substantial one. He gave me all his business after that. Other accounts were shaping up, too, and my efforts paid off in a salary increase. With this and my piano playing income, I was able to go to a Ford dealership that August and buy a brand new Model T on a Bohemian charge account—cold cash. I had been reading about the business boom down in Florida. Newspaper cartoons compared the rush down there to the gold rush of 1849, and I managed to talk Ethel into going down with me for the winter. She agreed to go if her sister, Maybelle, would come along. That was fine with me. The more the merrier, thought I.

Needless to say, my superiors at Lily Cup were more than happy to grant me a five months leave of absence. I went around to all my customers and told them nobody would be calling on them for five months, but I promised to be back in time to stock them up for the next summer season. Ethel and I stored our furniture, cranked up the Model T, and headed south on the old Dixie Highway. It was a memorable trip. I had five new tires when we left Chicago. When we arrived in Miami, not one of those originals was left on the car. It seemed like we averaged a blowout every fifteen or twenty miles. I'd jack up the car and pull off the wheel to patch the traitorous innertube, and sometimes while I was applying the glue or manning the air pump, another tire would go *bang!* and expire. The roads were pretty primitive, of course, especially those red clay tracks through Georgia. At one point we came to a washout where the road disappeared and was replaced by a hog wallow. Ethel held the baby in her lap and steered the car while her sister and I pushed, sinking knee deep in the red muck. Our struggles were vastly entertaining to a barefoot band of ragged children who gathered to watch. When we finally got through that one, I knew nothing could stop us.

Miami was packed to the rafters with fortune seekers like us, and we began to despair of ever finding a place to rest our weary heads. Finally, in a big old house smack in the middle of town, we found a kitchen and butler's pantry that had been furnished with a double bed, a single bed, a table, and a set of chairs. The rest of the house was filled with cots occupied by an assortment of male roomers, and the solitary bathroom in the place had to be shared with them. It was a place to stay, at least, and Ethel, bless her soul, didn't complain. Not at first. But it became increasingly difficult for her when her sister got an apartment of her own, a job as a secretary, and went her own way. I got a job with W. F. Morang & Son selling real estate for a development in Fort Lauderdale along Las Olas Boulevard. It was amazing. Everything I had been hearing about the real estate boom was true. The Company had twenty seven-passenger Hudson automobiles. If you got into the top twenty bracket in sales with them, you were given a Hudson and a driver for business use. That was for me, of course, and I made it quickly. I went to the Miami Chamber of Commerce and looked up the names of tourists who came from the Chicago area. I'd call them and fill them in—as one Chicagoan to another—on an exciting development I'd found in this palmy land of crazed speculation. They were all intrigued. I would take them by car up route A-1-A to Fort Lauderdale so they could see for themselves what was going on there along the "new river," the intercoastal waterway. The property was underwater, but there was a solid bed of coral rock beneath, and the dredging for the intercoastal raised all the lots high and dry, with permanent abutments. People who purchased those lots really got a bargain, even though the prices were astronomical for those times, because the area is now one of the most beautiful in all of Florida, and lots there are worth many times what they sold for then.

My job was to line up the prospects and get them to the property. There they would be taken on a tour of the development by a man we called the "spieler." We would follow along with them, and if we saw a couple begin to get glassy-eyed and ripe for the collar, we would signal another specialist who tagged along—the "closer." This gentleman would move in, and we would separate the marked couple from the rest of the herd and go to work on them. All it took to purchase one of these pieces of paradise was a $500 deposit. I got a number of deposits each trip. The people I was dealing with were mostly older folks. I felt that my twenty-three-year-old face was too callow to be credible for a real estate wheeler-dealer, so I decided to grow a mustache. It was a disaster. Most men have a margin around their lips, a demarcation where hair doesn't grow. I lack this feature, with the result that my mustache grew right down into my mouth. Moreover, it was a horrible brownish-red color. Ethel despised it, and I didn't like it much either. I didn't have to wear it long. The muckracking stories in northern newspapers soon pulled the plug on our big real estate boom, and there were no longer any prospects to worry about. What a colossal blow! Just when I was getting into the swing of selling these lots, the whole business vanished.

One morning I was sitting in the living room we all shared in our rooming house, noodling around on the decrepit old upright piano, and wondering what in the hell I was going to do next. I was seriously considering going back to Chicago and asking to get back on at the radio station and at the Lily Cup Company. My thoughts were so far away that at first I didn't notice the chap calling to me through the screen door. Finally I let him in, and he wanted to know if I'd like a job playing the piano.

"Is the Pope Catholic?" I replied.

He wanted to know if I had a tuxedo. I didn't, of course, but he allowed that a dark blue suit would do. That I had; and I could pick up a black bow tie on the way home from the union hall if they accepted my Chicago Musician's Union card and gave me a permit to play in Miami. I had to do some sight reading for the union tester, and then he asked me to play a tune I didn't know and transpose it into another key as I read it. My heart sank. I thought he was aiming to shoot me down and not give me a permit.

"Look, I can transpose a piece that I know," I said. "But if I have to sight read and transpose it at the same time I can't keep a tempo."

"That's all right," he said. "I just want to see if you know how."

"O.K., Mac. But this is going to be the groping method."

After a couple of tortured bars, he told me to stop and waved me back to the rear of the hall. I shot a despairing glance at my erstwhile employer and followed after the union man. To my immense relief, he wrote out a permit and handed it to me.

"That'll be five bucks," he said. Then he noticed my greenish pallor and said, "Hey, cheer up. You did fine. Your transposition was accurate, and that's all I ask."

The Florida sky looked bright again when we got outside, and I felt fine.

The job was with the Willard Robinson Orchestra in a plush nightclub on Palm Island called The Silent Night. Willard Robinson was a fine pianist himself, but he had a lot of personal problems at the time and was drinking heavily. After he fell off the piano stool a couple of times, the management told him he could keep leading the group, but he'd have to hire another piano player. His divorce and selling his house on Long Island (which he memorialized in his hit song of the day, "A Cottage for Sale") and his resultant drinking problem were to my benefit, of course. One man's famine makes another man's feast, and it's an ill wind that blows nobody good and all that. But subconsciously I felt a bit guilty about my good fortune at Willard's expense. I was happy to see him come back strong in New York a few years later. His Deep River Orchestra was featured on the original Maxwell House Showboat on radio, bringing his music the national audience it deserved.

The music we made at The Silent Night wasn't so bad either. Soon I was averaging $110 a week—good money in those days. At last we were able to move out of the rooming house into a three-and-a-half-room furnished apartment in a terrific new building.

My first night of playing at The Silent Night made quite an impression on me. The place itself was fabulous—gorgeous, glamorous, and illegal. The owner was a rum runner who brought the illicit booze he served from the Bahamas. A great hedge surrounded the place, and a doorman was posted at the entrance gate to screen guests as they arrived. Before opening the gate, I was told, the doorman would push one of two buttons. One would ring a bell that would bring the maitre d' bustling out to meet the patrons. The other button would sound an alarm that meant revenue agents. The doorman would delay the federal agents as long as he could. By the time they got inside there was no evidence of liquor in the place, except for a few drinks sitting in front of individual customers. If they tried to confiscate those, an angry argument would ensue about whether the prohibition law meant it was illegal to drink liquor or simply precluded its sale.

The bandstand was in an elaborate, rococo pavilion. The dance floor was of marble, surrounded by Grecian columns. One of the other guys in the orchestra pointed out a huge yacht tied to the dock and told me that it had once belonged to the Emperor of Japan. In inclement weather, the dining and dancing shifted to the yacht. I was astonished by the place and a bit cowed by the suave urbanity of the patrons. The drinks were a dollar each for anything you wished, champagne, brandy, bourbon, scotch, whatever. I didn't drink at all back then but the fixed-price drink menu and the stylish simplicity of the food service made a lasting impression on me. They had no printed menu because there were just three entrees: Maine lobster, steak, and roast duckling. Years later I recalled that spare bill of fare in my first motto for McDonald's—KISS—which meant, "Keep it simple, stupid."

Another thing that captivated me was the deft service of the Swiss waiters. They would bring out a roast duckling on a big wooden platter and filet it right at the customer's table, slicing it up with the flair of a magician producing rabbits from a hat. I admired their professionalism.

But I didn't have a lot of time to observe what was going on that first night. I played the piano continuously. When it came time to take a break, the rest of the players left the bandstand, but Robinson placed a silk top hat on the piano and told me I had to keep playing requests for people who wanted to sing. The customers tossed tips into the hat, and I felt good about that until I discovered that I was expected to share the tips with all the other players. That was grossly unfair, and I was steaming mad. But it was the custom, apparently, and there wasn't much I could do about it if I wanted to keep the job. I hammered away, my fingers getting painful from such unaccustomed exercise, and I vowed that I would figure out a way to keep this piano player from being the goat for the whole orchestra.

The solution didn't come to me that first night, or even the first week. I was too busy worrying about whether I would last the entire evening. When I'd get home my fingers would be puffed and almost bleeding, and I had to soak them in a bucket of warm water. I tried the direct approach to Willard Robinson once more on a night when he seemed relatively mellow and more sober than usual.

"Mr. Robinson, I think I am getting a dirty deal," I said. "When you played piano through all the breaks, it was different. You were the star folks had come to see, and they paid handsome tips. You could afford to share them, because you were getting your pay as leader, too. I'm just one of the boys, yet I have to play much more than the others and get nothing extra for it at all!"

He looked at me vacantly and then squinted until he got me in focus. "That's too bad, Joe," he responded. "Maybe you'll get smart and learn to play the flute or somethin'."

I got smart, all right, but no thanks to Robinson. I was doing my solo routine for requests one night, and an old geezer who'd won a bundle at the racetrack that day came in with a doll who could have been his granddaughter but obviously was not. They danced over to the piano in a spastic flutter, cheek-to-cheek, and the old boy waved a dollar bill at me and asked if I could play "I Love You Truly." I just stared at him and shook my head negatively. He was startled and the young girl slapped his hand with the dollar, knocking it into the top hat, and she shouted, "How dare you insult him with a dollar, you cheapskate!" Then she grabbed a twenty-dollar bill out of the bundle that protuded from his breast pocket and dropped it in my lap. "Hey, wait a minute," I called. "Did you say 'I Love You Truly'?" and I played the first few bars haltingly, as though striving to recall them. He nodded vigorously, and I went ahead with the tune and played the hell out of it. If my associates in the orchestra noticed the extra tip, they didn't say anything about it. Special requests for a little bit extra to the piano player became a common thing after that.

I got even smarter. I talked the violinist into playing the breaks with me and strolling through the audience, serenading each table individually. That doubled our tips immediately and was a big addition to our pay every week.

One night the revenue agents outmaneuvered the Palm Island security men and we all wound up in jail. I was mortified. My parents would disown me if they found out I had been put in jail with a bunch of common violators of the prohibition law. We were only there three hours, but it was one of the most uncomfortable 180-minute periods of my life.

That incident didn't cheer Ethel up at all either. We were doing well financially, and she even liked the apartment. But she was growing exceedingly homesick. At least when I was working all the time in Chicago, she'd had her family and friends to keep her from being too lonely. Here, she had no one at all. Her sister was dating, leading her own life, and they seldom saw each other. So the warm weather was cold comfort for Ethel. Finally we agreed to go back to Chicago. Our lease on the apartment ran until March 1, but Ethel couldn't wait that long. I put her and the baby on the train about the middle of February and stayed alone to play out my two weeks' notice so the orchestra could get a replacement for me.

That long drive home alone in my Model T was an unforgettable experience. I caught snatches of sleep along the road from time to time, but aside from that, I drove straight through. I had no top coat, and the weather got increasingly colder as I drove north. When I reached Chicago's southern limits, the streets were covered with ice. At Sixty-third and Western, the car went into a skid, and I ended up on the curb on the wrong side of the street. A big policeman came rushing over swearing at me, sitting there shivering in my light suitcoat, "What's the matter," he yelled. "Are you drunk?" I was afraid I was due for another few hours in jail, but I explained my plight and he let me go. Like most Chicagoans, he figured anyone who'd been taken in the Florida real estate scandal was a damned fool, but more to be pitied than scorned.

My parents' home never looked more welcome than it did that day. Ethel fed me hot soup and got me into a warm bed, and I slept for fifteen hours straight.

I had left Florida in the nick of time, it turned out. The business decline that began when the real estate boom collapsed caught up with the nightclubs soon after I left. The Silent Night closed its gates for good. Palm Island popped into the news once in a while as time went by. Al Capone built a home there. Then Lou Walters, father of TV's Barbara Walters, opened the Latin Quarter. But it was to be a long time before I saw Florida again.

4

The ten years between 1927 and 1937 were a decade of destiny for the paper cup industry. It was exciting to watch the business grow. But if I had known the disillusionment that was waiting for me, I might have gone into some other line of work.

When I returned to selling paper cups, I vowed that this was going to be my only job. I was going to make my living at it and to hell with moonlighting of any kind. When I played the piano, it would be for pleasure only. I intended to devote every ounce of my energy to selling, and that's exactly what I did.

My boss was a shrewd operator named John Clark, a man who could recognize sales talent when he saw it. I didn't see his true colors for several years, after he made a bargain with me that the devil himself would have been proud of. Clark was president of Sanitary Cup and Service Corporation, whose biggest stockholders were a pair of bachelor brothers in New York by the name of Coue. This corporation was the exclusive Midwest distributor for Lily brand cups, which were manufactured by Public Service Cup Company. They made cups in several different sizes, from one ounce on up to sixteen ounces. These

were rather primitive containers by today's standards. The larger
ones had to be pleated and then coated with paraffin wax to make
them rigid enough to hold liquids, and they had rims that were
limp and floppy.

I peddled these cups all over Chicago. I sold lots of the smaller
sizes to Italian pushcart vendors who filled them with flavored ice
and sold one ounce for a penny, two ounces for two cents, and five
ounces for a nickel. They called them "squeeze cups" because you
would squeeze the bottom and force the ice up to lick it. I sold
soft drink cups to concessions at Lincoln Park and Brookfield
zoos, to beaches, racetracks, and, of course, to the baseball parks.
I used to needle my friend Bill Veeck up in Wrigley Field, trying
to get him to stock more cups for Cub games. Bill wasn't very
promotion minded in those days. He became a much different
guy when he owned the baseball teams himself. I was always on
the lookout for new markets, and I found them in some strange
places. Italian pastry shops, for example, could be sold "squat-
size" cups for pastry and spumoni. They would buy a lot of them
for big picnics, weddings, and religious festivals. I also learned
that Polish places in the old Lawndale neighborhood would buy
the same cups to serve "Povidla," which was a prune butter.
Those folks ate an awful lot of prune butter.

America had become an ice cream society in the last years of
the Twenties, thanks in large part to Prohibition. Bars and fine
lounges in hotels sold ice cream, because they could no longer sell
liquor, and dairy bars began to crop up all over the country. It
was an incredible era. The straitlaced Cal Coolidge, who assured
the nation that his fiscal probity had brought prosperity here to
stay, moved the White House to the Black Hills of South Dakota
for the summer and celebrated the Fourth of July by parading
around in a cowboy costume. Babe Ruth signed a three-year
contract with the Yankees for the stupefying figure of $70,000 a
year. Lindbergh flew nonstop from New York to Paris. Al Jolson
sang in the first talking pictures. And—wonder of wonders—in
1929 the Chicago Cubs won the National League pennant!

Big things were happening in the paper container industry. A
paper milk bottle called the Sealcone was introduced by a New
York dairy. Sealcone had no closure, the housewife had to snip

off the top with a scissors, so it didn't drive glass bottles from the nation's doorsteps as predicted. But the same technology that produced the Sealcone, using paraffined spruce fiber, was utilized by the makers of Tulip cups. When that firm merged with Lily Cup in 1929, it gave me a "straight-sided" cup that was much more rigid and adaptable to other container uses. It allowed me to go after sales to coffee vendors and cottage cheese packers. The merger of Lily and Tulip was wonderful, a big step forward. The year's most notorious event, however, took the entire country several giant steps backward. It was the stock market crash, which ushered in the Great Depression.

My father was one of the large losers in the economic collapse. After he had given up his position in New York in 1923 and returned to Chicago, taking a demotion to please my mother, he began working out his frustrations by speculating in real estate. That was probably the fastest-building bubble in the whole inflation-bloated country. Newspapers and magazines in the late Twenties were full of advertisements for correspondence courses that were guaranteed to help you get rich quick in real estate. My father didn't need to take any of those courses. He owned property scattered all over northeastern Illinois. I remember that he bought a corner lot on Madison Street in Oak Park one month and sold it to an automobile dealership the following month at a handsome profit. The real astonisher, however, was a lot he bought in Berwyn for $6,000 and sold a short time later for $18,000!

Father seemed to have a Midas touch when it came to picking property. He was so busy pyramiding his land holdings, though, that he somehow failed to see—as we all failed to see—whatever warnings there might have been of the impending crash. When the market collapsed, he was crushed beneath a pile of deeds he could not sell. The land they described was worth less than he owed. This was an unbearable situation for a man of my father's principled conservatism. He died of a cerebral hemorrhage in 1932. He had worried himself to death. On his desk the day he died were two pieces of paper—his last paycheck from the telegraph company and a garnishment notice for the entire amount of his wages.

Another piece of paper discovered among my father's effects was a yellowed document dated 1906. It was a phrenologist's report of a reading he had done on the bumps on the head of Raymond A. Kroc, aged four. He had predicted that I would become a chef or work in some branch of food service. I was amazed at the prognostication; after all I was in a food-service-related business and felt a real affinity for kitchens. Little did I know how much more accurate that old boy's prophesy would eventually prove to be.

In 1930 I made a sale that not only gave Lily Tulip Cup Company a big boost in volume but also gave me an insight into a new direction for paper cup distribution. I was selling our little pleated "souffle" cups to the Walgreen Drug Company, a Chicago firm that was just starting a period of tremendous expansion. They used these cups for serving sauces at their soda fountains. Observing the traffic at these soda fountains at noon, I perceived what I considered to be a golden opportunity. If they had our new Lily Tulip cups, they could sell malts and soft drinks "to go" to the overflow crowds. The Walgreen headquarters was at Forty-third Street and Bowen Avenue at that time, and there was a company drugstore just down the street. I presented my pitch to the food service man, a chap named McNamarra. He shook his head and threw up his hands at my suggestion.

"You're crazy, or else you think I am," he protested. "I get the same fifteen cents for a malted if it's drunk at the counter, so why the hell should I pay a cent and a half for your cup and earn less?"

"You would increase your volume," I argued. "You could have a special area at the counter where you would sell these things, put covers on them, and take them and the same vanilla wafers or crackers you serve with them at the fountain and drop them in a bag to take out."

Mac's face got redder than usual at that and he rolled his eyes toward heaven as if pleading to be delivered from this madman. "Listen, how can I possibly make a profit if I go to this extra expense? Then you want me to waste my clerk's time putting covers on drinks and stuffing them in bags? You are dreaming."

One day I said, "Mac, the only way in this world that you can increase your soda fountain volume is to sell to people who don't take up a stool. Look, I'll tell you what I'm gonna do. I will *give* you 200 or 300 containers with covers, however many you need to try this for a month in your store down the street. Now most of your takeout customers will be Walgreen employees from headquarters here, and you can conduct your own marketing survey on them and see how they like it. You get the cups free, so it's not going to cost you anything to try it."

Finally he agreed. I brought him the cups, and we set the thing up at one end of the soda fountain. It was a big success from the first day. It wasn't long before McNamarra was more excited about the idea of takeouts than I was. We went in to see Fred Stoll, the Walgreen purchasing agent, and set up what was to be a highly satisfactory arrangement for both of us. The best part of it for me personally was that every time I saw a new Walgreen's store going up it meant new business. This sort of multiplication was clearly the way to go. I spent less and less time chasing pushcart vendors around the West Side and more time cultivating large accounts where big turnover would automatically winch in sales in the thousands and hundreds of thousands. I went after Beatrice Creamery, Swift, Armour, and big plants with in-factory food service systems such as U.S. Steel. I sold them all, and my success brought me more territory to cover and more possibilities.

One day an order was sent down from Lily Tulip's headquarters in New York that because of the depression everyone was obliged to take a ten percent pay cut. In addition, because prices had dropped on gas, oil, and tires, all car allowances would be cut from fifty dollars a month to thirty dollars.

I was then sales manager and John Clark called me into his office to give me the news.

"Close the door, Ray, I want to talk privately with you," he said. Then he told me how much he appreciated my hard work, how well the company thought of my production, but I would have to take a salary and expense cut. It applied to everyone, across the board.

This was a real blow. It wasn't the reduction in salary that bothered me, but the affront to my ego. How could they treat the best salesman they had in this arbitrary fashion? I knew how much money I was making for them, depression or not, and I felt cold fury rising in me. I looked at him for a long minute, and then I said, very quietly, "Well, I'm sorry, but I can't accept that."

"Ray, you have no alternative."

Now, when I get excited or agitated, my voice goes up in register and in volume. I was really agitated now.

"The hell I don't have an alternative," I yelled. "I'm quittin'. I'm giving two weeks' notice right now, and if you want me to leave today, I'll leave today."

Mr. Clark was shaken by my outburst, but he managed to keep his voice fairly steady. "Come on now, Ray. Calm down. You're not going to leave and you know it. This is too big a part of your life. It is your life. You belong here with your company and your men."

I tried to control my temper. "I know it's my life . . ." I started; then my voice went up again, "But goddammit, I'm not going to hold still for this. When times were good I got little enough in the way of rewards . . . ." Now I was shouting again. "Unacceptable. This is unacceptable, that I be put on the same basis with some of the people who are cost problems to the corporation. Those people—you know who they are—they're part of the overhead in this company. I'm part of the creative. I bring in the money, and I'm not gonna put myself in the same category with them!"

"Ray, listen a minute. I'm taking a cut myself."

"Take it. That's your prerogative. Take it, brother, but I won't accept it. I will not!"

I knew he must have been squirming inside, imagining the sound of our voices carrying through the walls to the horrified secretaries and clerks in the outer office. But I didn't give a damn, and the more he tried to soothe me and assure me that the policy was designed to provide the greatest good for the greatest number, to protect all our jobs while times were bad, the madder I got. The capper was when he said that after I thought it over I would understand that it was the only fair way to handle it.

"I can understand it, perfectly," I said as I stood up to walk out of the office. "But I refuse to accept it. This company has already squeezed me out of pennies. Now, the minute things get a little tough, I'm supposed to sacrifice dollars. Well, I'm not doing it. You can have your damned job with its ten percent pay cut. I'm quittin' and that's that."

When I left the office that day, I took my sample case with me. I said nothing to my wife about what had occurred. I knew how upset she would be if she learned I had quit my job. To her, what I had done would be indefensible. I'm hotheaded and proud, and I felt my action was justified. I was a little frightened about my future, but I concealed it and acted as though nothing had happened.

Each morning I left home at the usual time, carrying my sample case. I would ride the elevated train to a corner in the Loop where there was an automat I used as a headquarters for reading through want ads over a cup of coffee. Then I'd set out on the day's round of job interviews.

I was looking for work that offered something more than money, something I could really get involved in. But there were no jobs of any kind, it seemed. There were a dozen or more men for every opportunity, if one can stretch that word to cover the most mundane tasks. I felt some of the starch begin to seep out of me after three or four days, but I was determined that I would never go back to Lily Tulip hat in hand. After about the fourth day of this, when I went home, my wife greeted me with a look that would have withered crabgrass.

"Where have you been?" she demanded.

"What do you mean, where have I been?"

"Mr. Clark called here. He wants to know where you are."

"Where am I?"

"Ray, don't be funny. Something's fishy here. I told him you are going in every morning, but he said he hasn't seen you for the last four days. Don't you go into the office every morning? What are you doing? What's going on?"

I hemmed and hawed about taking some "future orders," but I wasn't very convincing.

"Well, Mr. Clark said he wants to see you first thing in the morning," she said. "You will be there, won't you?"

I felt trapped. I hated being put on the defensive. I walked away, but she kept after me like the determined Scot she was, telling me to answer her. So I whirled around and let her have it.

"I can't take those cheapskates down there any more," I blurted. "I'm quittin'!"

Zingo! Her jaw dropped. Her eyes widened. Then she really lit into me. I was betraying her and our daughter. My pride was jeopardizing our existence. She stormed on about my foolishness, how desperate times were, how difficult it was for anyone to find a job (I *knew* that!). But I had taken my stand. I wasn't going to back down, regardless. I couldn't. Everything in me resisted it.

"Ethel, honey," I said soothingly, "don't worry. I'll find something. We'll get by. I'll go back to playing the piano if I have to."

That was the wrong thing to say. She had spent too many nights alone while I was off playing piano someplace. I was afraid she was going to go into hysterics, so I agreed to go in and see John Clark the next morning.

When I walked into his office, Clark looked at me with alarm and shouted, "Where have you been?"

"I've been out looking for another job. I told you, I am not going to stay here."

"Oh, come on, Ray. Close the door. Sit down. You can't leave here. This is where you belong. Admit it. You love your work and you know it."

"Yes, I do know it. But I can't put up with the kind of treatment I'm getting. I simply will not stand for it."

"This is only a temporary thing, Ray, just until times get better. Can you afford to be so independent?"

"According to my wife, I can't. But I am. I take the cut as an insult, and I'm not going to be insulted."

He walked to the window and looked out, hands shoved into his pockets, and was silent for several minutes. Finally, he turned to me and said, "Okay. Give me a couple of days to see what I can work out. Do your job as though nothing had happened. I'll let you know in two or three days."

"That's fine with me. Two or three days."

Late in the afternoon of the third day, he called me in again.

"Close the door and sit down," he said. "Now, Ray, this is absolutely confidential. Here's what we'll do. I've made arrangements for you to get a special expense account that will make up for the ten percent salary cut. It will include the payment balance on your car of $20 a month. Now . . . will you stay?"

"Thank you very much," I said. "On that basis I'll stay."

I felt several inches taller when I left that office. I'd won! This was going to be a fine prize to lay at Ethel's feet.

Of course, the implication of the whole affair was that I would have to work harder than ever and produce more sales for the company. I did it gladly. Clark never told me so, but I knew as time went on that he was well aware that he had made a good deal. We had other run-ins from time to time, usually because of my insistence on protecting my customers. Most of these people trusted me enough that when I went into their stores, they'd simply wave and smile and go on waiting on customers. I would go to their stockrooms and see what their supply of paper cups was like. If they needed more, I'd order them. For the big-volume customers, I made certain they didn't lose by dealing with me instead of a competitor.

I'd tell them, "Look, I think you'd better stock up on paper cups. I believe there's going to be a price increase. I have nothing official, of course, or I wouldn't be able to tell you about it. But there's something in the wind, and I think your prices are going to be going up."

When Clark found out about that, he was madder than a hornet. But it didn't cost Lily Tulip anything. They had warehouses full of cups made at the existing prices, and it certainly built good will among my customers.

I had about fifteen salesmen working for me then, and we had a fine spirit of enthusiasm percolating among us. After work we would get together and talk shop, batting around ideas about how to sell more paper cups. That was fun. I loved to see one of these young fellows catch hold and grow in his job. It was the most rewarding thing I'd ever experienced. I wasn't much older than any of them, and some were older than me. But I felt like a father to them.

It got to the point in the office that I was generating too much business, too much paperwork, to be handled by the clerical pool, so Mr. Clark told me I should hire a secretary.

"I suppose you're right," I said. "But I want a male secretary."

"You what?"

"I want a man. He might cost a little more at first, but if he's any good at all, I'll have him doing a lot of sales work in addition to administrative things. I have nothing against having a pretty girl around, but the job I have in mind would be much better handled by a man."

That set off another series of arguments and closed-door sessions. But finally I won my point. A young fellow named Marshall Reed came in off the street one day looking for a job. He'd gone to business school in California and had come to Chicago hoping to get work at a newspaper. That didn't pan out, so he wandered into our office, and he was sent to me because the people out front knew that I was getting ready to place a classified ad for a male secretary. I liked Reed because he was honest and leveled with me from the start.

"I can type 60 words a minute and take shorthand at 120 words a minute," he told me solemnly, "but this is my first experience outside of school. I don't know anything about your business."

"Don't worry about it," I said. "I'll explain what I'm doing as we go along. If you have any questions, just ask me."

It wasn't long before he was a real working member of my team. My decision to hire a male secretary paid off when I was hospitalized for a gall bladder operation and later for a goiter operation. Marshall worked between our office and my hospital room, and we kept things humming as briskly as when I was in the office every morning.

We were doing well despite the depression. I had bought a Buick automobile, which I got secondhand for about the same price I would have had to pay for a new Model-A Ford, and I shined it up until it looked like it had just rolled out of the factory. Ethel's Scotch thrift and my Bohemian prudence meshed well, and our savings grew steadily. We were able to afford a live-in maid now, a girl we hired for $4 a week plus room and board. We treated her like part of the family.

I took care not to be ostentatious (I detest snobs), but my style kind of dazzled my staff at the office. They were eager to follow my examples. I stressed the importance of making a good appearance, wearing a nicely pressed suit, well-polished shoes, hair combed, and nails cleaned. "Look sharp and act sharp," I told them. "The first thing you have to sell is yourself. When you do that, it will be easy to sell paper cups." I also counseled them on handling money, encouraging them to spend wisely and save some for a rainy day.

One morning as I was sending the boys out for a day of selling, I got a call that I was to report to Mr. Clark's office. When I walked in he looked at me darkly, ignoring my friendly greeting.

"Close the door, Ray, I have a very serious matter to discuss with you."

When I was seated, he leaned back in his chair and glared at me over tented fingertips.

"I hear that you've been telling your salesmen how to make money on their expense accounts."

"That's right," I said. "I have."

"Get out!" he exploded. "Get out of here and stay out!"

I nodded and walked carefully to the door. I put my hand on the knob and turned slowly to face him. It was deathly still, and I think he was feeling shocked at his own abruptness.

Our eyes locked and I said, "May I say something?"

He nodded grimly.

"Here is exactly what I told my men: Each of you gets a certain amount per diem for your expenses on the road. You get so much for a room, so much for travel, and so much for food. Instead of staying in a room with a bath, take a walk down the hall. You'll be just as clean, and you'll save some money. When you take the train, get an upper berth, you'll sleep just as well as in a lower and it will cost you less. Don't eat breakfast in the fancy hotel restaurant, go to the YMCA cafeteria. Have prunes and oatmeal; it's filling and it's good for you; it keeps you being a regular guy."

By this time, Mr. Clark was grinning in embarrassed relief. He couldn't say anything. He just turned his palms up and waved me out. I walked away feeling tall again, although I had half a notion to quit over his unjust accusation.

My battles with the boss were beginning to get me down, and I might have told him to go to hell once and for all if I hadn't been having so much fun selling. There were interesting developments popping up all over. An engineer from Sterling, Illinois, named Earl Prince had a coal and ice business he was phasing out, and he was building little castles in towns all around Illinois in partnership with a boyhood buddy of his named Walter Fredenhagen.

They called them Prince Castle ice cream parlors, and they sold cones and bulk ice cream and a few sundaes, for which they bought paper cups from me. I kept my eye on them, I thought their operation had a lot of promise.

Over in Battle Creek, Michigan, I had a customer named Ralph Sullivan who had put a dairy bar up in front of his creamery, and he had invented a drink that was pulling in an astounding business. Ralph had come up with the idea of reducing the butterfat content in a milk shake by making it with frozen milk. The traditional method of making a shake was to put eight ounces of milk into a metal container, drop in two small scoops of ice cream, add flavoring, and put the concoction onto a spindle mixer. Ralph's formula was to take regular milk, add a stabilizer, sugar, cornstarch, and a bit of vanilla flavoring and freeze it. The result was ice milk. He would put four ounces of milk in a metal container, drop in four scoops of this ice milk, and finish it off in the traditional way. The result was a much colder, much more viscous drink, and people loved it. The lines around his store in the summertime were nothing less than amazing. This ice-milk shake had a lot of advantages over regular milk shakes. Instead of being a thin, semicool drink, it was thick and very cold. Since it had substantially less butterfat, it could be digested more easily, or as we say in the food service business, it *wore* better: People didn't go around belching and burping for half an hour after drinking one. I was selling Ralph Sullivan a lot of paper cups. This started in about 1932, and it kept growing and growing until I was selling him 100,000 sixteen-ounce cups at a time.

Walter Fredenhagen was running the Prince Castles in my area from his office in Naperville. I'd never met Earl Prince. But I started working on Walter, trying to talk him into looking at Ralph Sullivan's operation.

"Ray, you are a nice guy, and I like you. But I do not want to get into the milk shake racket," he said. "We do a nice clean ice cream trade here, and the last thing I want is a big clutter of milk bottles to handle. It's too messy."

"Walter, I am amazed that a forward-looking guy like you who keeps himself informed about the dairy business can be ignorant of the latest developments," I said. "Now they are making a milk dispenser that takes a five-gallon can and keeps it refrigerated.

You draw the milk from a spigot just like draught beer. You can make the ice milk in your plant right here in Naperville. It's cheaper than making ice cream, and you'll see profits you never dreamed possible."

At last, one day, Walter talked it over with Earl Prince, and they agreed to drive into Chicago and meet me. Then I'd drive them over to Battle Creek. We would return that same evening. I liked Earl immediately. He was a very plain-spoken, straightforward guy. In later years the girls in my office would laugh about his frugality. Here was this highly successful, wealthy man who wore a musty old hat and somewhat seedy looking clothes. He could afford to take the entire staff out to lunch at the Pump Room, but he steadfastly refused to pay Chicago restaurant prices—any restaurant. Instead, he'd send out for a peanut butter sandwich. I never knocked his frugality, of course; I respected it although he may have carried it to extremes.

Both Earl and Walter had their eyes opened on that trip to Battle Creek. They were sold on the frozen-milk shake and wanted to start with their own version immediately. The whole trip back to Chicago was spent planning for the new operation with the shake that Earl announced he was going to call the "One-in-a-Million." As they chattered on about it, I waited for my opportunity to put in an idea of my own.

"It sounds great," I said at last, "but there is one thing I want you to do."

"What is it?" asked Earl expansively.

"I want you to charge twelve cents for this drink instead of a dime."

"Huh?" I could tell that both of them were genuinely flabbergasted.

"That's right. Sell it for twelve cents. You'll still be giving people a hell of a value, and it will actually increase interest and sales."

"Ray, I respect your ability as a salesman," Walter said gently. "But obviously you are out of touch with the retail end. People just don't want to be bothered with extra change, counting pennies, you see? It is a big inconvenience for a cashier, too. So forget it."

That taken care of, they were prepared to go on talking about other matters in setting up "One-in-a-Million." But I kept insisting on the twelve-cent price, and it caused a pretty heated discussion. Finally Earl turned around to Walter and said, "Son of a bitch, I am going to teach this guy a lesson! I'm going to sell it for twelve cents in our first store and let him watch the thing fall on its face. Then, when we get it perfected, we can go into all the stores and sell it for a dime." Walter didn't answer. I think I'd worn them out.

The record books of Prince Castles show that they did indeed start selling the "One-in-a-Million" at twelve cents. They never reduced the price. It took off like a barn fire. Earl Prince was not unhappy that he failed to teach me a lesson, either. I sold him five million sixteen-ounce cups that first year, so by adding on the two cents as I insisted, he made an extra $100,000.

That kind of volume made Earl Prince's creative juices start flowing. Prince Castle mixed shakes ahead and kept the sinks full of metal containers being rinsed. During busy periods, it was almost impossible to keep up with the demand for metal cans. Earl invented a collar made from the upper half of a metal shake can. The cylinder had been compressed or tapered at the bottom, and he took a sixteen-ounce paper cup and fitted the metal ring on top of it. The tapered part extended down into the paper cup like a sleeve. The upper portion sat on the rim of the cup, extending up to make the whole thing exactly the same height as a regular metal can—six and seven-eighths inches. He demonstrated it to me by putting together a "One-in-a-Million" shake in a paper cup with the metal collar and stuck it on the mixer. It worked!

I needed no further demonstration. It all fell into place in my mind. It was sensational for sure. Not many days later, we had a supply of metal sleeves at the Lily Tulip office in Chicago, and I demonstrated the idea for John Clark and the other company executives. They loved it, especially when I showed them how I intended to merchandise it to owners of dairy bars and soda fountains. I would go into a place and explain how I could save them some money with these metal sleeves for their Lily Tulip cups. I would buy ten milk shakes—ten metal cans full—and pour them out for people as I talked about how tasty and refreshing and wholesome this drink was. I'd make the waitress leave the metal cans standing on the counter while we finished off our drinks. All this time, of course, the residue was melting in the metal cans. When we finished, I'd grab a sixteen-ounce cup from my sample case and proceed to drain each metal can into it. The result was another full cup of milk shake! In practice that rarely failed to convince the owner. From then on, he used metal sleeves, and Lily Tulip cups—no more metal cans.

This new method stepped up Prince Castles' sales volume so much that their single-spindle Hamilton Beach mixers could no longer handle it. The "One-in-a-Million" was a heavier drink to begin with, and when the mixers were run continuously they simply burned out. That situation is what inspired Earl Prince to invent the Multimixer. At first this machine had six spindles arranged around the central pedestal stand and the top could be rotated to take the drinks off. But that resulted in too many dropped drinks and other minor disasters, so the top was made stationary and the spindles reduced to five. This machine was powered by a one-third horsepower, industrial-type electric motor with direct drive. There were no carbon brushes to wear out. You could mix concrete with the damn thing if you had to. This was the invention that really made big volume milk shake production possible, and it changed the course of my life.

After Earl had the Multimixer in production, I took one of the machines down to the Lily Tulip office and held another demonstration. John Clark was knocked cold by it, and we got busy and signed a contract that made Sanitary Cup and Service Corporation the exclusive distributor of the Multimixer. I felt like Lindbergh and Admiral Perry all rolled into one—a real hero.

Strangely enough, however, the Lily Tulip headquarters in New York wanted no part of it. In fact, they complained that they had been getting calls from customers in other parts of the country wanting to know about metal milk-shake cup sleeves and "Multiple Mixers" or some such thing, and they declared that they were not about to become jobbers for some mixer maker in the Midwest. They were manufacturers of paper cups, and that is what they intended to remain. I could scarcely believe it. I knew we had barely dented the potential market for Multimixers.

Earl Prince proposed that I leave Lily Tulip and go into

business with him. I would market the inventions he came up with, starting with the Multimixer. I'd be the sole agent for Multimixer in the country. He'd manufacture the things, I'd handle the accounts receivable, and we'd split the profits. It sounded very tempting. I was getting more and more fed up with Lily Tulip. I was about to lose one of my biggest accounts, Walgreens, the people I had created a tremendous amount of business for and to whom I was selling five million cups a year. Fred Stoll told me in strictest confidence that a former Walgreen executive who had a lot of pull in the top offices of the company had gone into the paper cup business with a competitor of mine, and he was going to be given all of the Walgreen trade. The rationale would be that this competitor was selling for five percent under my price. I explained this to John Clark and tried to get him to go along with offering Walgreens a price break—after all, they paid their bills on time and there was promotion value in having a big company like that use your product. But all I got was a tongue lashing. He said I was no longer a salesman; my customers were selling me! I was smoldering after that.

Ethel was incredulous at the idea that I would give up my position at Lily Tulip and go off on a flyer like this. We had just moved into a fine home in a project named Scarsdale in Arlington Heights, northwest of Chicago. We were extremely comfortable there. Ethel loved it, and she felt threatened by this proposal. "You are risking your whole future if you do this, Ray," she said. "You are thirty-five years old, and you are going to start all over again as if you were twenty? This Multimixer seems good now, but what if it turns out to be just a fad and fails?"

"You just have to trust my instincts," I said. "I am positive this is going to be a winner. Besides, Earl will come up with a lot of other marketable ideas. This is just the beginning. I want you to help me; come down and work in the office for me and together we will make it a terrific business."

"I will do no such thing."

"But Ethel. I need your help. You know I can't afford to hire someone, and it would be good for you, for both of us. Please?"

She absolutely refused to help. I'm sure she felt justified, but I felt betrayed. I just couldn't believe she'd let me down like that. She wouldn't even agree to work part-time or for a limited period, until I got the business going. That was when I began to understand the meaning of the word *estrangement.* It is a terrible feeling, and once it appears, it grows like dry rot.

My disappointment with Ethel did not deter me, though. When I have my mind made up about a business deal, that's it. I was going to move ahead regardless. However, I had not even considered the kind of problems I would encounter with Mr. John Clark when I tried to extricate myself from Lily Tulip Cup. This time, I closed the door to his office without being told. He looked at me owlishly and said, "Yes?"

"J. A., I am going to resign. I am going to be the exclusive sales agent for the Multimixer. That's good for you because it gets me out of your hair, and I am going to sell a hell of a lot of paper cups for you when I start putting Multimixers in stores all over the country."

"You can't do that, Ray," he said, as if he were talking to a child and patiently explaining some important but obvious thing. You *do not have* the Multimixer contract. Sanitary Cup and Service Corporation has it."

"Well, what the hell, you can give it up. You've told me repeatedly that you are not going to get into Multimixer sales yourselves. And you know that what I said is true, I am going to sell a good many million paper cups for you."

"You don't understand. The Coue brothers would never give it up. You don't know how they operate."

"Listen, they have to!" I brought this thing in here in the first place out of loyalty to you and to the Coues and the company. I didn't have to do that. If you were using it, that would be one thing, but the company doesn't want it. Give it back to me. You can't put a thing like this on the shelf, it won't sit there, it's too big!"

I was controlling myself as well as I could, but Clark could see that I was getting ready to blow a gasket, so he said, "Well, let me talk to them and see what we can work out."

What he worked out was a deal in which I got the Multimixer

contract, and Sanitary Cup got sixty percent of my new company, which I named Prince Castle Sales. It was a satanic setup, but I didn't see that then. It was the only way out, it seemed, and I had to take it. And, at any rate, the corporation would put up $6,000 of the $10,000 capital I needed to get started, so it didn't seem such a big handicap. But it was soon to become an anchor chained around my neck.

5

There's almost nothing you can't accomplish if you set your mind to it.

I told that to a group of graduate students at Dartmouth College in March 1976. They had asked me to address them on the art of entrepreneurship—how to pioneer a business venture. "You're not going to get it free," I said, "and you have to take risks. I don't mean to be a daredevil, that's crazy. But you have to take risks, and in some cases you must go for broke. If you believe in something, you've got to be in it to the ends of your toes. Taking reasonable risks is part of the challenge. It's the fun."

I was having a lot of fun back in early 1938 when I struck off on my own with a brand-new Multimixer in a big sample case and the whole nation of soda fountain operators and restaurant owners quivering in anticipation for this product. At least I thought they were. It didn't take long for me to discover how wrong I was on that score.

A fellow who already had six single-spindle machines would look down his nose at my gleaming, thirty-pound metal mush-

room and tell me that he couldn't see putting all his drinks on one
mixer. If it burned out, he'd be out of business until it could be
repaired. With six individual machines, on the other hand,
chances of all of them burning out at once were slim. And even
with three or five of them out of commission, he'd still be able to
make a malt. That point of view was a mighty tough one to
change. I butted heads with a lot of flinty operators. Some of
them I was able to convince, others never saw the light. But there
was enough evidence of interest to maintain my faith in the
product. I believed it would be successful.

I was a one-man marching band. I had a tiny office in the
LaSalle-Wacker Building in Chicago, but I was seldom there. My
secretary ran the office while I traveled all over the country. Sales
were not bad, considering the newness of the product. I could feel
it beginning to catch on. But I was extremely unhappy with my
financial setup. As sixty-percent partner, Sanitary Cup was able to
restrict my salary, and John Clark kept it at the same level I'd
been at when I left Lily Tulip Cup. I determined after a little over
two years that I was going to have to get that sixty percent back
somehow. So I went to Clark and broached it to him. It was then
I learned how he'd misled me. The Coue brothers had given up
their interest to him. They probably never cared about Multimixer at all, and he was going to take his pound of flesh from my
heart. I was boiling mad, but there was not a damn thing I could
do about it.

"I think this machine you're selling has a big future, Ray," he
said. "I was willing to discount the present to allow you to realize
that future. But if you insist on getting my share back, then I must
tell you that I want a handsome return on my capital investment."

Never mind that I hadn't wanted his damned capital in the first
place, and neither had Earl Prince.

"All right," I said, "how much?"

I don't know how he kept from choking on his own bile as he
mouthed the figure: *"Sixty-eight thousand dollars."*

That's all I remember of our conversation. I'm sure I said
something. But I was so benumbed by his outrageous demand
that I couldn't think straight. To add acid to the irony, he wanted
the whole thing in cash. Of course, I didn't have that kind of

money. So what we worked out was the culmination of the devilish deal he had tied me to. I had to agree to pay him $12,000 cash. The balance was to be paid off over five years, plus interest. My salary had to remain at the same level and my expenses in the same range. So, in fact, what I was doing was paying him the profits of my company.

I didn't know where in the hell I was going to raise the money, but I had made up my mind to do it. In the end, most of the cash came from my new home in Arlington Heights. I managed to get an increase in the mortgage, much to Ethel's dismay. Her apprehensions about my becoming Mr. Multimixer had been laid to rest at this point, and I don't think she ever got over the shock of discovering that we were nearly $100,000 in debt. She couldn't seem to handle it.

For me, this was the first phase of grinding it out—building my personal monument to capitalism. I paid tribute, in the feudal sense, for many years before I was able to rise with McDonald's on the foundation I had laid. Perhaps without that adversity I might not have been able to persevere later on when my financial burdens were redoubled. I learned then how to keep problems from crushing me. I refused to worry about more than one thing at a time, and I would not let useless fretting about a problem, no matter how important, keep me from sleeping. This is easier said than done. I did it through my own brand of self-hypnosis. I may have read a book on the subject, I don't remember, but in any case I worked out a system that allowed me to turn off nervous tension and shut out nagging questions when I went to bed. I knew that if I didn't, I wouldn't be bright and fresh and able to deal with customers in the morning. I would think of my mind as being a blackboard full of messages, most of them urgent, and I practiced imagining a hand with an eraser wiping that blackboard clean. I made my mind completely blank. If a thought began to appear, zap! I'd wipe it out before it could form. Then I would relax my body, beginning at the back of my neck and continuing on down, shoulders, arms, torso, legs, to the tips of my toes. By this time, I would be asleep. I learned to do this procedure rather rapidly. Others marveled that I could work twelve or fourteen hours a day at a busy convention, then entertain potential customers until two or three o'clock in the morning, and still be out of bed early, ready to collar my next client. My secret was in getting the most out of every minute of rest. I guess I couldn't have averaged more than six hours of sleep a night. Many times I got four hours or less. But I slept as hard as I worked.

There was a lot of nervous tension at that time on all levels of society over the alarming developments in Europe and Asia. Magazines speculated grimly on whether war with Japan was inevitable. Then our attention was diverted from Japanese aggression in China to the Nazi conquests in Europe. On December 7, 1941, we were thrown into war by the Japanese sneak attack on Pearl Harbor, and I was thrown out of the Multimixer business. Supplies of copper, used in winding the motors for Multimixer, were restricted by the war effort.

A salesman without a product is like a violinist without a bow. So I scratched around and made a deal with Harry B. Burt to sell a line of low-fat malted milk powder and sixteen-ounce paper cups for a drink called Malt-a-Plenty. It was mixed in the cup, using the metal sleeve or collar, just like One-in-a-Million. I kept needling Earl Prince to come up with some new ideas for me to sell, but it seemed as though he could think of nothing that wasn't illegal or rationed. I managed to make a living on Malt-a-Plenty, but paying off my debt to John Clark became a real nightmare. I did it, though, and when World War II ended I was able to go back to selling Multimixers as my own. It was a glorious feeling.

Business recovered after the war, and soon it was better than ever. New soft-mix ice cream purveyors were starting up as franchises, and I was in there pushing Multimixers into this expanding market, to Dairy Queen, Tastee-Freeze, and the rest. I sold a Multimixer to a guy named Willard Marriott, who had just opened a drive-in called A & W Root Beer. His method of operation fascinated me. I considered myself a connoisseur of kitchens; after all, selling Multimixers took me into thousands of them. I prided myself on being able to tell which operations would appeal to the public and which would fail. Willard Marriott looked like a winner to me from the start. I had no more idea than he did back then, though, of what a giant his Marriott Corporation would become in hotels and restaurants. I was spending a lot of time in bars in those days, too. Not as a customer, but as a critic. The whole mixed-drink industry seemed entirely too bland to me. It needed livening up with new drinks that used ice cream. They would be mixed, of course, on a Multimixer. My favorite concoction was brandy or creme de menthe, crème de cacao, or Kahlua with ice cream. The result was a soft custard that could be both an after dinner drink and dessert. I called the thing the *Delacato*. One place, the Evergreen, a well-known steak house in Dundee, Illinois, served the Delacato in a champagne glass, to be eaten with a spoon or sipped through a little straw. Obviously, my invention did not alter the nation's drinking habits, but it was an interesting notion.

My pattern of travel in peddling Multimixers hinged around the restaurant and dairy association conventions. I hit all of their national shows and the larger regional ones as well. I would order a dozen or so Multimixers to be sent to each show by Railway Express from our plant in downstate Illinois. When I arrived, I would display some of them in my own booth and set the others on the counters of the big manufacturers of soda fountains, Liquid Carbonic, Bastion-Blessing, Grand Rapids Soda Fountain, and others. I never left one of those shows without selling all of my samples, in addition to other orders. That's why I dreaded the last day of any show. I'd have to repack the machines for shipment to the purchasers. I've never been handy with tools, and crating those machines was always an interlude spiced with splinters, skinned knuckles, and plenty of profanity. It was worth the irritation, naturally, but I sometimes wished I'd gotten into selling something I could fit in my pocket. My sample case for the Multimixer weighed close to fifty pounds. I had wheels installed on the bottom of it so I could pull it down the street like my little red wagon. But it was a hassle to get it in and out of taxicabs or up a long flight of stairs.

I didn't bother setting sales goals for Multimixer. I didn't need any artificial incentives to keep me working at top speed. My estimate of when I was having a good year was when I sold 5,000 units. I had several of those. One year—1948 or 1949—I sold 8,000.

That kind of volume was making my style of operating from

outside the office increasingly difficult. I needed more help. But I was reluctant to hire another office worker. It was useless to ask Ethel to come in, she had made that perfectly clear. Yet it didn't seem to me that the business was strong enough to add another hand. Finally, late in the fall of 1948, my accountant, Al Doty, convinced me that I was going to have to hire a bookkeeper. I respected Al's judgment. He had been recommended to me by my friend Al Handy at Harris Trust & Savings Bank, and his firm handled my accounting for many years. Anyhow, Al got me going and I put an ad in the papers. I can't remember how many girls I interviewed, but I'll never forget the brilliant waif who got the job. There was no question in my mind after we talked for a few minutes that this Mrs. June Martino was the one to hire. She was wearing a faded coat that hardly looked adequate for the December storm that was whipping down the LaSalle Street canyon that day, and she looked as though she'd missed several meals. Yet she had a presence that conveyed integrity and a restless native ability to deal with problems. This was enveloped in a warm, compassionate personality, a rare combination of traits. The fact that she had no bookkeeping experience bothered me not at all. I knew she would master the technical routines quickly. So I told her I couldn't pay much, but if she was willing to work hard anyhow, I could promise her a bright future. We talked the same language. She did work hard—unbelievably hard—and in less than twenty years she was one of the top women executives in the country, secretary and treasurer of McDonald's Corporation.

June came from an improvident German family on the northwest side of Chicago. She and Louis Martino were married shortly before World War II. He was an engineer with Western Electric, and the company wanted to have him exempted from the military draft because he was working on a coaxial cable invention that could be vital to defense communications. One day June took some papers down to the army personnel office that was processing Louis's classification. When she left, he had been exempted from the service, but she had been sworn in! She was very patriotic and just got carried away. As a WAC she studied electronics at Northwestern University and learned trigonometry and calculus and God knows what else. She had to do it by intensive tutoring, because she had no special aptitude for higher mathematics. But that's the sort of person she was; no challenge was too big for her. If she didn't know something, she'd burrow into library books and find out.

June had a couple of children toward the end of the war; then her father and Louis's mother both became seriously ill. Soon they were $14,000 in debt. They decided to move the whole shooting match, in-laws, kids, and the two of them, to a farm near the Wisconsin Dells. Housing was cheap up there, and they figured they could raise a lot of their own food. Louis planned to get a job in a television repair shop and work the farm, too. A lot of young couples were doing that sort of thing at the time. It may have panned out for a few of them, but many more, the Martinos among them, found they couldn't make it go. Louis couldn't afford to leave his job to look for work in Chicago, so June came down and stayed with a friend while she haunted the employment agencies. That's how she happened to walk into my office that bitter cold December day.

A charming thing about June was that despite her solid business sense, she was absolutely innocent about money matters. She also had a remarkable intuition. It bordered on the psychic at times, and she had a childlike faith in it. I saw it work the first day she was in my office. I sent her over to the bank to make a deposit. She had exactly twenty cents, as she explained later, and that was her carfare home. But she passed a Salvation Army band playing on the corner, and something in her heart would not let her go by with that money in her purse. So she tossed the two dimes into the kettle and went on to the bank. When she got back to the office, she was ecstatic.

"Oh, Mr. Kroc, what a wonderful day this is! I got this job, and it's my little boy's birthday. He's still up on the farm, of course, and I was wishing I could buy a present to send him but it seemed impossible." She then went on to tell me about having only twenty cents to her name and how she'd tossed it into the Salvation Army kettle. As she left the bank, coming back to the office, her heel caught in a sidewalk grating. She looked down to dislodge it, and there, next to her foot, was a twenty-dollar bill! "I went back into the bank and asked the tellers if they had any idea who had lost it. One of them looked at me and said, 'Lady, I think you really ought to keep it.' Can you imagine such luck?"

That's typical of the kind of thing that happened to June. I thought it was good to have a lucky person around, maybe some of it would rub off on me. Maybe it did. After we got McDonald's going and built a larger staff, they all called her "Mother Martino." She kept track of everyone's family fortunes, whose wife was having a baby, who was having marital difficulties, or whose birthday it was. She helped make the office a happy place.

It wasn't easy to be cheerful about my business in the early 1950s. Al Doty once told me that he liked to have lunch with me because he always learned something about his own business trends. "You seem to be able to see further into the future than the rest of us," he said. I believe I did. And what I saw made me very unhappy. It was clear that Multimixer's days were numbered. Liquid Carbonic Corporation's stockholders had engaged in a big proxy fight. The man who had inherited the presidency was determined to continue the firm's manufacture of soda fountains out of dedication to employees who had served that division loyally for many years. His opponents wanted to scrap the soda fountain division, because it was losing money. They won. Other manufacturers were cutting back, too. The handwriting was on the wall, and Walgreen's underscored it when, for the first time, they began pulling soda fountains out of their stores.

The upshot of all this, I knew, was that I had to find a new product. Preferably something that would be as innovative and as attractive as Multimixer had been fifteen years earlier. I thought I had it in a unique folding kitchen table and benches that a neighbor of one of my salesmen had made. The idea appealed to me, so I went out to the man's home to see it. The table and benches folded up into the wall like an ironing board. It seemed like a great spacesaver for small kitchens. I had Louis Martino construct a model for me. It looked great. I had some reservations about it, but my anxiety to get a new product for my salesmen to market overcame my doubts. I gave it the name "Fold-a-Nook" and had the sample shipped to the Beverly Hills

Hotel in California, where I intended to introduce it with a big splash.

All the top developers and builders I'd invited for the occasion came and sipped cocktails in the elegant room I'd rented. They admired the fresh flowers and praised the hors d'oeuvres. The party was a terrific success, but "Fold-a-Nook" was an enormous flop. I got not a single order.

I might have pursued that project, disappointed though I was at the lack of response in California, but I learned that unbeknown to June Martino and me, the salesman who had put me onto the thing was conspiring with my secretary to pirate the "Fold-a-Nook" from me. I fired both of them on the spot. Their rejoinder was to copy the "Fold-a-Nook" and bring it out under another name. That man had been a fellow worker and golfing companion since Lily Tulip Cup days; I had loaned him money for the down payment on his house. So I took no pleasure in the fact that they later went broke. By the same token, however, I wouldn't listen for a moment when he called later to plead for a chance to get into McDonald's. A good executive does not like mistakes. He will allow his subordinates an honest mistake once in a while, but he will never condone or forgive dishonesty.

It was not long after the "Fold-a-Nook" fiasco that I became intrigued by the stories of the McDonald brothers and their operation that kept eight Multimixers whirring up a bucket brigade of milk shakes out there in sunny San Bernardino. "What the hell," I thought, "I'll go see for myself." So I booked my fifty-two-year-old bones onto the red-eye special and flew west to meet my future.

6

In the early 1930s in Southern California there developed a remarkable phenomenon in the food service business. It was the drive-in restaurant, a product of the Great Depression's crimp on the free-wheeling lifestyle that had grown up around movie-happy Hollywood. Drive-ins sprouted in city parking lots and spread along highways and canyon drives. Barbecue beef, pork, and chicken were the typical menu mainstays, but there was an endless variety in service approaches as feverish operators hustled to outdo one another. Aspiring starlets worked as carhops, glad of any opportunity that would help them pay the rent and exhibit their charms at the same time. The drive-in operators cooperated by competing to see who could come up with the most exciting carhop costume. One of them had his girls zooming around his parking lot on roller skates.

Into that strange scene came my future mentors in the hamburger business, the McDonald brothers, Maurice and Richard, a pair of transplanted New Englanders. Maurice had moved out to California in about 1926 and got a job handling props in one of the movie studios. Richard joined him after he was graduated from West High School in Manchester, New Hampshire, in 1927. Mac and Dick worked together in the studio, moving scenery, setting up lights, driving trucks, and so forth until 1932, when they decided to go into business for themselves. They bought a run-down movie theater in Glendora. It provided a very sparse living, and Mac and Dick perfected the art of squeezing the bejesus out of every penny. They sometimes ate only one meal a day, and often that was a hot dog from a stand near their theater. Dick McDonald recalls that watching the owner of that hot dog stand, who had one of the few places in town that seemed to be doing any business, was probably what gave him and his brother the idea of going into the restaurant field.

In 1937 they talked the owner of a lot in Arcadia, near the Santa Anita racetrack, into putting up a small drive-in building for them. They knew nothing about food service, but they had a man who was experienced as a barbecue cook, and he showed them the ropes. Obviously, they picked it up pretty fast. Two years later they were scouting around the railroad town of San Bernardino looking for a location for a bigger barbecue operation. A fellow named S. E. Bagley from the Bank of America got them started with a $5,000 loan.

The San Bernardino restaurant was a typical drive-in. It developed a terrific business, especially among teenagers. But after World War II, the brothers realized they were running hard just to stay in one place. They weren't building volume even though their parking lot was always full. So they did a courageous thing. They closed that successful restaurant in 1948 and re-opened it a short time later with a radically different kind of operation. It was a restaurant stripped down to the minimum in service and menu, the prototype for legions of fast-food units that later would spread across the land. Hamburgers, fries, and beverages were prepared on an assembly line basis, and, to the amazement of everyone, Mac and Dick included, the thing worked! Of course, the simplicity of the procedure allowed the McDonalds to concentrate on quality in every step, and that was the trick. When I saw it working that day in 1954, I felt like some latter-day Newton who'd just had an Idaho potato caromed off his skull.

So I asked Dick McDonald—when he wondered aloud who they'd get to open a lot of similar restaurants for them—"What about me?" The response seemed to surprise him and his brother momentarily. But then they brightened and began discussing this proposal with increasing enthusiasm. Before long we decided to get their lawyer involved and draw up an agreement.

In the course of this conversation I learned that the brothers had licensed ten other drive-ins, including two in Arizona. I had no interest in those, but I would have rights to franchise copies of their operations everywhere else in the United States. The buildings would have to be exactly like the new one their architect had drawn up with the golden arches. The name, McDonald's, would be on all of them, of course, and I was one hundred percent in favor of that. I had a feeling that it would be one of those promotable names that would catch the public fancy. I was for the contractual clauses that obligated me to follow their plans down to the last detail, too—even to signs and menus. But I should have been more cautious there. The agreement was that I could not deviate from their plans in my units unless the changes were spelled out in writing, signed by both brothers, and sent to me by registered mail. This seemingly innocuous requirement created massive problems for me. There's an old saying that a man who represents himself has a fool for a lawyer, and it certainly applied in this instance. I was just carried away by the thought of McDonald's drive-ins proliferating like rabbits with eight Multimixers in each one. Also, I was swayed by the affable openness of the McDonald brothers. The meeting was extremely cordial. I trusted them from the outset. That trust later would turn to bristling suspicion. But I had no inkling of that eventuality.

The agreement gave me 1.9 percent of the gross sales from franchisees. I had proposed 2 percent. The McDonalds said, "No, no, no! If you tell a franchisee you are going to take two percent, he'll balk. It sounds too full and rounded. Make it one and nine-tenths, and it sounds like a lot less." So I humored them on that one. The brothers were to get .5 percent out of my 1.9 percent. This seemed fair enough, and it was. If they had played their cards right, that .5 percent would have made them unbelievably wealthy. But as my Grandpa Phossie used to say, "There's many a slip twixt the cup and the lip." Another aspect of the agreement was that I was to charge a franchise fee of $950 for each license. This was to cover my expenses in finding a suitable location and a landlord who would be willing to build to our specifications. Each license was to run for twenty years. My contract with the McDonalds was only for ten years. That was later amended to ninety-nine years.

I've often been asked why I didn't simply copy the McDonald brothers' plan. They showed me the whole thing and it would have been an easy matter, seemingly, to pattern a restaurant after theirs. Truthfully, the idea never crossed my mind. I saw it through the eyes of a salesman. Here was a complete package, and I could get out and talk up a storm about it. Remember, I was thinking more about prospective Multimixer sales than hamburgers at that point. Besides, the brothers did have some equipment that couldn't be readily copied. They had a specially fabricated aluminum griddle for one thing, and the set-up of all the rest of the equipment was in a very precise, step-saving pattern. Then there was the name. I had a strong intuitive sense that the name McDonald's was exactly right. I couldn't have taken the name. But for the rest of it, I guess the real answer is that I was so naive or so honest that it never occurred to me that I could take their idea and copy it and not pay them a red cent.

I was elated with the deal I'd struck, and I wanted to tell someone about it right away, so I dropped in to visit Marshall Reed, my former secretary at Lily Tulip Cup. Marsh had served in the army during World War II. He went back to selling paper cups for a time after the war, but then he married a wealthy widow and retired to California. He was glad to see me, as always, and we had an interesting talk about my new venture. Since I was committed to it, he didn't tell me what was really on his mind until years later: "I thought you'd gone soft in the head . . . was this a symptom of the male menopause? . . . I asked myself, 'What is the president of Prince Castle Sales doing running a fifteen-cent hamburger stand?' " Good old Marsh. He'd never step on another man's happiness.

Others were less kind.

Ethel was incensed by the whole thing. We had no obligations that would be jeopardized by it; our daughter, Marilyn, was married and no longer dependent on us. But that didn't matter to Ethel; she just didn't want to hear about the McDonalds or my plans. I had done it again, and once too often as far as she was concerned. The quarrels we'd had when I took over Prince Castle and then when I'd extended the mortgage on our house to buy out John Clark were mere preludes to this one. This was a veritable Wagnerian opera of strife. It closed the door between us. She dutifully attended McDonald's gatherings in later years, and she was liked by operators' wives and by women on the staff, but there was nothing more between us. Our thirty-five years of holy matrimony endured another five in unholy acrimony.

I had no time to bother with emotional stress, though. I had to find a site for my first McDonald's store and start building. I needed to get a location that I could establish as a model for others to follow. My plan was to oversee it in my spare time from the Prince Castle business. That meant it would have to be situated near my home or near my office, and downtown Chicago was impossible for a number of reasons. Finally, with the help of a friend named Art Jacobs, who went in fifty-fifty with me on it, I found a lot that seemed just right. It was in Des Plaines, a seven-minute drive from my home and a short walk from the North-western Railroad Station, from where I could commute to the city.

My troubles started the minute I got together with my contractor and went over with him the plans furnished by the McDonald's architect. That structure was designed for a semi-desert location. It was on a slab, no basement, and it had a swamp cooler on the roof.

"Where am I going to put the furnace, Mr. Kroc?" he asked.

"Damned if I know. What do you suggest?"

He suggested a basement, pointing out that other arrangements would be far less efficient and that I would need a basement for storage anyhow. I couldn't just leave my potatoes outdoors as the McDonalds did, for example, and there was no room for a back building on this lot, even if I'd wanted one, which I didn't.

So I called the McDonald boys and told them about my problem.

"Well, sure you need a basement," they said. "So build one."

I reminded them that I had to have it documented by a registered letter. They pooh-poohed it; said it was all right to go ahead, they weren't much good at writing letters and they couldn't afford to hire a secretary. Actually they probably could have hired the entire typing pool at IBM if they'd had a mind to. I hung up hoping that they would have second thoughts and send me written confirmation, but they never did.

It was a messy way to start, being in default on the first unit, but there was no choice. I went ahead with the building, telling myself that when I got breathing space I would fly out to see the McDonalds and get all the contractual wrinkles ironed out at once. That would have worked, had the McDonalds been reasonable men. Instead, they were obtuse, they were utterly indifferent to the fact that I was putting every cent I had and all I could borrow into this project. When we sat down with our lawyers in attendance, the brothers acknowledged the problems but refused to write a single letter that would permit me to make changes.

"We have told you by telephone that you may go ahead and alter the plans as we discussed," said their attorney, Frank Cotter.

"But the contract calls for a registered letter. If Mr. Kroc does not have that, he is put in jeopardy," said my counsel.

"That's your problem."

It was almost as though they were hoping I would fail. This was a peculiar attitude for them to take because the more successful the franchising, the more money they would make. My attorney gave up on the situation. I hired another and he quit, too, saying I was plain crazy to continue under such conditions. He could not protect me if the McDonalds should close in on me. So I said, "Let 'em try," and I plunged ahead.

My home in Arlington Heights was right next to Rolling Green Country Club where I belonged and where I had a lot of business friends and golfing companions. Most of these locker-room acquaintances shared the general opinion that I had taken leave of my senses in getting into this fifteen-cent hamburger business. But I had one close friend who was quite interested in the venture. He had a son-in-law named Ed MacLuckie who was looking for a job and who had expressed a liking for the food service business. Ed was working a wholesale hardware territory over in Michigan at the time and it was not going well. So I talked to him. He was one of these whip-lean, nervous types who are often very fussy and fastidious and have great endurance. Just the kind of qualifications I was looking for, so I hired him as a manager of my first store. Art Bender, the McDonald brothers' manager, came to Des Plaines and helped Ed and me open that store on April 15, 1955. It was a hell of an ordeal, but the experience was to prove invaluable in opening other stores. Incidentally, Art Bender is still with us. He's a highly successful operator in California. So is Ed, who has stores in Michigan and Florida.

My notion about using that first unit as an experimental model was a good one. It took nearly a year to shake it down into a smooth-running operation although it made money from the start. I probably wouldn't have been able to get the thing started if it hadn't been for Jim Schindler of Leitner Equipment Company. He went out to San Bernardino and studied the layout of the griddles, fry vats, and so forth in the McDonald brothers' store. Then he adapted them to my plans in Des Plaines. One of the things I did differently was to make my milkshakes with a soft product drawn from a tank, instead of hand-dipping ice cream. This changed the layout and gave us more space. One major problem in adapting the California-style building to the midwestern climate was ventilation. I brought in architectual consultants one after the other in an attempt to solve the problem of exhausting the stale air and replacing it with fresh cool or heated air. These guys could design a cathedral, but they didn't seem to be able to deal with my little hamburger store. It gets pretty cold in April in the Chicago area, so our furnace was put into action right away. The problem was that the fans for the griddle and fry vats would exhaust all the heat the furnace was putting out and continually blow out the pilot light. This could have allowed gas to accumulate dangerously. The temperature inside the store would hover around forty degrees. As the weather warmed up, the reverse happened, cool air was exhausted, allowing the inside temperature to climb up to around a hundred degrees.

A subject of much greater concern to me, however, was the great french-fry flop. I had explained to Ed MacLuckie with great pride the McDonald's secret for making french fries. I showed him how to peel the potatoes, leaving just a bit of the skin to add flavor. Then I cut them into shoestring strips and dumped them into a sink of cold water. The ritual captivated me. I rolled my sleeves to the elbows and, after scrubbing down in proper hospital fashion, I immersed my arms and gently stirred the potatoes until the water went white with starch. Then I rinsed them thoroughly and put them into a basket for deep frying in fresh oil. The result was a perfectly fine looking, golden brown potato that snuggled up against the palate with a taste like . . . well, like mush. I was aghast. What the hell could I have done wrong? I went back over the steps in my mind, trying to determine whether I had left something out. I hadn't. I had memorized the procedure when I watched the McDonald's operation in San Bernardino, and I had done it exactly the same way. I went through the whole thing once more. The result was the same—bland, mushy french fries. They were as good, actually, as the french fries you could buy at other places. But that was not what I wanted. They were not the wonderful french fries I had discovered in California. I got on the telephone and talked it over with the McDonald brothers. They couldn't figure it out either.

This was a tremendously frustrating situation. My whole idea depended on carrying out the McDonald's standard of taste and quality in hundreds of stores, and here I couldn't even do it in the first one!

I contacted the experts at the Potato & Onion Association and explained my problem to them. They were baffled too, at first, but then one of their laboratory men asked me to describe the McDonald's San Bernardino procedure step-by-step from the time they bought the potatoes from the grower up in Idaho. I detailed it all, and when I got to the point where they stored them in the shaded chicken-wire bins, he said, "That's it!" He went on to explain that when potatoes are dug, they are mostly water. They improve in taste as they dry out and the sugars change to starch. The McDonald brothers had, without knowing it, a natural curing process in their open bins, which allowed the desert breeze to blow over the potatoes.

With the help of the potato people, I devised a curing system of my own. I had the potatoes stored in the basement so the older ones would always be next in line for the kitchen. I also put a big electric fan down there and gave the spuds a continuous blast of air, which greatly amused Ed MacLuckie.

"We have the world's most pampered potatoes," he said. "I almost feel guilty about cooking them."

"That's all right, Ed, we're gonna treat 'em even better. We're gonna fry 'em twice," I told him. I explained the blanching process the potato people had recommended we try. We gave each basket of fries a preliminary dip in the hot oil and let them drip dry and cool off before cooking them all the way through. Finally, about three months after we'd opened the store, we had potatoes that measured up to my expectations. They were, if anything, a little better than those tasty morsels I'd discovered in San Bernardino. We worked it out so the blanching was done on a regular production-line basis. We'd take two baskets at a time and blanch them for three minutes. They would be a rather unappealing gray color when they came out at that point, but the cooling and draining would allow some oil to penetrate into the body of the potato. The chemistry of this tinge of oil in the starch of the morsel when it was dumped back to fry for another full minute created a marvelous taste. They'd emerge for the second time golden, glowing, and appealing. We would dump them into a stainless steel drain pan under a few heat lamps and let the grease drain off. Then they would be placed, with sugar tongs, two or three strips at a time, into the serving bag. That process wouldn't work today. It would be far too costly in labor. Even then a lot of people marveled that we could sell those potatoes for a dime.

One of my suppliers told me, "Ray, you know you aren't in the hamburger business at all. You're in the french-fry business. I don't know how the livin' hell you do it, but you've got the best french fries in town, and that's what's selling folks on your place."

"You know, I think you're right," I replied. "But, you son of a bitch, don't you dare tell anyone about it!"

I was elated when I finally got that store open and it began to show a profit. I recognized that it was not in the best of all possible locations; at most it was a mediocre site for a place that had no prior public exposure. Yet it was doing well, and I was able to move ahead and start lining up my franchisees for other locations. The first place I looked for them was the locker room at Rolling Green, and many of my golfing friends became very successful McDonald's operators.

Then the whole deal ground to a halt on another piece of dramatic deviousness or dumbness, I don't really know which, on the part of the McDonald brothers.

I had been made aware of the ten other sites in California and Arizona that the brothers had lent their names to, and we'd agreed that was fine. I was to have all of the rest of the United States. But there was one other agreement they hadn't told me about, and that was for Cook County, Illinois, where I had my home, my office, and my first model store. The brothers had sold Cook County to the Frejlack Ice Cream Company interest for $5,000!

It cost me $25,000 to buy that area from the Frejlacks, and it was blood money. I could not afford it. I was already in debt for all I was worth.

I couldn't blame the Frejlacks, of course, they were completely above board and fair. But I could never forgive the McDonalds. Unwittingly or not, they had made an ass of me—in the Biblical sense. I'd been blindfolded by their assurances and led to grind like blind Samson in the prison house.

My only salvation was the good will I'd built up over the years in Prince Castle Sales. The income from Multimixer paid the rent and all salaries while I was slaving away to get McDonald's started. I would drive down to Des Plaines each morning and help get the place ready to open. The janitor would arrive at the same time I did, and if there was nothing else to be done, I'd help him. I've never been too proud to grab a mop and clean up the rest rooms, even if I happened to be wearing a good suit. But usually there were a lot of details to be taken care of in terms of ordering supplies and keeping the food operation going, so I would write out detailed instructions for Ed MacLuckie concerning them. Ed came in about 10 o'clock in the morning to open the store at 11 o'clock. I would leave my car at the store and walk the three or four blocks to the Northwestern station, where

I'd catch the 7:57 express to Chicago and be in my Prince Castle office before 9 o'clock.

June Martino was usually there ahead of me and had the day's business started with our East Coast reps. I had manufacturers' representatives all over the country to handle Multimixer sales. For a time I kept some of the big customers, such as Howard Johnson's, Dairy Queen, and Tastee Freeze, as my personal accounts. I relinquished these gradually as McDonald's business demanded more and more of my attention. In the evenings, I would commute back to Des Plaines and walk over to the store. I was always eager to see it come into view, my McDonald's! But sometimes the sight pleased me a lot less than other times. Sometimes Ed MacLuckie would have forgotten to turn the sign on when dusk began to fall, and that made me furious. Or maybe the lot would have some litter on it that Ed said he hadn't had time to pick up. Those little things didn't seem to bother some people, but they were gross affronts to me. I'd get screaming mad and really let Ed have it. He took it in good part. I know he was as concerned about these details as I was, because he proved it in his own stores in later years. But perfection is very difficult to achieve, and perfection was what I wanted in McDonald's. Everything else was secondary for me.

7

Harry Sonneborn.

That name on my appointment calendar in late May of 1955 was familiar yet strange. I remembered having talked to him on the telephone a few times about Multimixer sales when he was vice-president of Tastee-Freeze. Now he'd called to tell me he had resigned from Tastee-Freeze, sold all his stock, and he wanted to come to work for me.

"I heard about your operation in Des Plaines, so I went out to look it over," he said. "I can tell just by watching it from across the street that you've got a winner there, Mr. Kroc, and I'd like to be part of your organization."

"Call me Ray," I told him. "I'd be interested in chatting with you, but I must tell you that I'm not in a position to hire anyone."

"I'd like to try and change your mind about that, Ray," he said. So we arranged a time to meet in my office.

Truthfully, I knew I needed help. But I also knew that I couldn't afford it. Prince Castle Sales was funding my entire operation, paying my salary and that of June Martino in addition to most of the costs involved in setting up my new franchise system. Then I had the added burden of buying out the Frejlack interest in Cook County, to the tune of $25,000. My share of the profit from the Des Plaines store, after splitting with Art Jacobs, didn't leave much. Moreover, from my experience in opening that store, I could foresee that unless I moved a lot faster, expenses were going to gobble up my $950 license fees long before a franchise could complete its building, generate business, and start returning 1.9 percent of its sales to me. I was spreading myself far too thin as it was, so the only way to speed up the franchising process would be to hire someone to help. I was damned if I did, doomed if I didn't.

Harry Sonneborn was thirty-nine years old when he came in to see me. He was almost six feet but looked taller, because of a kind of awkward, Lincolnesque angularity about him. He wore his hair cropped in a German military cut that suited the disciplined intensity of his manner. We found that we talked the same language concerning the franchise business and its potential. Obviously, as Harry said, it was a business fraught with a great deal of danger. Developing a franchise system and enforcing high standards would be difficult. Also, of course, there was the growing specter of government regulation. As we discussed these things, it became evident to me that Harry was exactly the man I needed to help me get McDonald's going. The problem remained, though, as I explained to him once more, that I could not afford to hire him. His answer was that he would go home and figure out the lowest possible salary he could take and still be able to support his family; then he'd get back to me.

I had to admire his persistence, and also the resolve he had that he would devote every working minute to McDonald's—twenty-four hours a day if necessary. I believed him. It was exactly the way I felt, and June Martino, too.

All my thoughts led to the conclusion that I had to hire Harry. I could visualize him handling finance while June ran the office and I was responsible for operations and new development. With that sort of setup, we could move ahead rapidly, which was the only way to go. In the first place, I had to mobilize my franchise sales and start generating some cash flow. Secondly, I was in the field by myself at the moment, but I knew that others would soon be jumping in to compete, and I wanted to take full advantage of my head start.

In a few days, Harry called back and said he could come to work for $100 a week take-home pay. It was an offer I couldn't refuse. Good thing for McDonald's that I didn't, because the company could never have grown as it did without the unique vision of Harry Sonneborn.

Harry was born in Evansville, Indiana. His parents died when he was very young, and he was brought up by an uncle who had a men's clothing factory in New York. Harry loved New York City. He grew up there in that climate of reverence for literature and art that is typical of so many Jewish families. But somehow, after college at the University of Wisconsin, he landed in Chicago to stay. He never lost that New Yorker aloofness, though, and this made me bristle sometimes. Yet I had to admire the way he studied the legal and financial problems we were steaming into. He immersed himself in stacks of books and learned the ins-and-outs of contracts and financial maneuvers as well as the lawyers and the bankers. We were breaking new ground, and we had to make a lot of fundamental decisions that we could live with for years to come. This is the most joyous kind of executive experience. It's thrilling to see your creation grow. It's dangerous, of course, because a small mistake can be absolutely ruinous. But in my definition, an executive is a person who rarely makes mistakes.

One of the basic decisions I made in this period affected the heart of my franchise system and how it would develop. It was that the corporation was not going to get involved in being a supplier for its operators. My belief was that I had to help the individual operator succeed in every way I could. His success would insure my success. But I couldn't do that and, at the same time, treat him as a customer. There is a basic conflict in trying to treat a man as a partner on the one hand while selling him something at a profit on the other. Once you get into the supply business, you become more concerned about what you are making on sales to your franchisee than with how his sales are doing. The temptation could become very strong to dilute the quality of what you are selling him in order to increase your profit. This would

have a negative effect on your franchisee's business, and ultimately, of course, on yours. Many franchise systems came along
after us and tried to be suppliers, and they got into severe business
and financial difficulty. Our method enabled us to build a
sophisticated system of purchasing that allows the operator to get
his supplies at rock-bottom prices. As it turned out, my instinct
helped us avoid the anti-trust problems some other franchise
operations got into.

Another judgment I made early in the game and enforced
through the years was that there would be no pay telephones, no
juke boxes, no vending machine of any kind in McDonald's
restaurants. Many times operators have been tempted by the side
income some of these machines offer, and they have questioned
my decision. But I've stood firm. All of those things create
unproductive traffic in a store and encourage loitering that can
disrupt your customers. This would downgrade the family image
we wanted to create for McDonald's. Furthermore, in some areas
the vending machines were controlled by the crime syndicate, and
I wanted no part of that.

Our first three franchises were sold in Fresno, Los Angeles, and
Reseda, California. Those stores opened in the year after the Des
Plaines operation got started. It was easier to swing deals in
California, because landlords could be shown the successful
operation the McDonald brothers had in San Bernardino and,
consequently, were more readily persuaded to put up our kind of
building for lease to my franchisees. It was painfully slow going,
like trying to ice skate on bare concrete, but we worked like mad,
and in the last eight months of 1956 we opened eight stores, only
one of them in California. The first franchise in the Midwest was
in Waukegan, Illinois, a city on the shore of Lake Michigan about
forty miles north of Chicago. It was an incredible experience.
The landlord was a banker, and he was very skeptical about the
prospects of our fifteen-cent hamburger business. He really didn't
think our operator would be able to make the rent. The
franchisee was doubtful, too. I asked Ed MacLuckie to go up and
help open the store, and he ordered all the supplies. Before long I
got a phone call from the operator, and he was madder than a
hornet. "You guys are trying to ruin me!" he yelled. "MacLuckie

has got more meat and buns in this place than I'll be able to use in a month . . . ." My, how he raged! But that store took off like a barn fire the day it opened, May 24, 1956, and Ed had to make a panic run back to the Des Plaines store to borrow enough meat and buns to get Waukegan through the weekend. The operator, needless to say, was happy to eat his words. The owner of the real estate however, was convinced that I'd pulled a fast one on him. I don't think a day of that twenty-year lease passed that he didn't wish he'd demanded a lot more. Of course, beyond my faith in the fast-food concept, I had no better idea than he did about how the location was going to do. I've always dealt fairly in business, even when I believed someone was trying to take advantage of me. That's one reason I have had to grind away incessantly to achieve success. In some ways I guess I'm naive. I always take a man at his word unless he's given me a reason not to, and I've worked out many a satisfactory deal on the strength of a handshake. On the other hand, I've been taken to the cleaners often enough to make me a certified cynic. But I'm just too naturally cheerful to play that role for long, even after dealing with the likes of Clem Bohr.

Clem was one of the more charming con men I met when we were building McDonald's. He was a contractor from Wisconsin, and he had approached Harry Sonneborn with a proposal that sounded rather appealing. Bohr said he wanted to travel around and find good locations for McDonald's restaurants in different parts of the country. He would purchase the land and have his firm erect a building on it, which he would then lease to us. We agreed, and Bohr marched off into the suburbs of distant cities to look for land.

Harry and I gave little further thought to Clem Bohr, because we were too busy with our own projects. The biggest of these was the move that made possible McDonald's dramatic growth. It started our evolution as a company whose business was developing restaurants and selling franchises to operate them.

We agreed that we wanted McDonald's to be more than just a name used by many different people. We wanted to build a restaurant system that would be known for food of consistently high quality and uniform methods of preparation. Our aim, of course, was to insure repeat business based on the system's reputation rather than on the quality of a single store or operator. This would require a continuing program of educating and assisting operators and a constant review of their performance. It would also require a full-time program of research and development. I knew in my bones that the key to uniformity would be in our ability to provide techniques of preparation that operators would accept because they were superior to methods they could dream up for themselves. But research and development and a staff to supervise and service operators effectively takes money.

The experience of Tastee-Freeze and Dairy Queen, two prominent franchising firms in the country at that time, and our own sense of direction with the units in California led to the conclusion that the only practical way for McDonald's to grow as we envisioned would be for us to develop the restaurants ourselves. Being in the restaurant development business would mean that we could plan a strong system in which locations could be developed by McDonald's as part of an overall, long-range, nationwide marketing program.

That idea was exciting, wow! It appealed to my salesman's instinct, because, obviously, it would make the right to operate a McDonald's restaurant far more valuable to a potential operator than if we were franchising only a name. But building dream castles was one thing; actually getting into the restaurant development business was a seemingly insurmountable problem. Harry's solution, the formation of Franchise Realty Corporation, was to my mind a stroke of financing genius.

Franchise Realty was the supreme example of a guy putting his money where his mouth is. I did a lot of talking about the ideal way to develop McDonald's with the kind of quality and uniformity that would insure our success. And when Harry came up with a way to make it possible, I backed it by going into hock for everything I had—my house, my car, you name it. Talk about grinding it out! I felt like Samson with a fresh haircut. But that dream of what the company could be sustained me.

We started Franchise Realty Corporation with $1,000 paid-in capital, and Harry parlayed that cash investment into something like $170 million worth of real estate. His idea, simply put, was that we would induce a property owner to lease us his land on a subordinated basis. That is, he would take back a second mortgage so that we could go to a lending institution (in the early days it was a bank) and arrange a first mortgage on the building; the landlord would subordinate his land to the building. I must admit that I was a bit skeptical: Why would a landlord want to do that? But I let Harry plunge ahead without interference.

I believe that if you hire a man to do a job, you ought to get out of the way and let him do it. If you doubt his ability, you shouldn't have hired him in the first place. I knew that Harry had schooled himself thoroughly in the fundamentals of leasing agreements. In addition to the volumes he pored over, he hired a consultant from Washington, D.C., an expert in real estate deals named Dreyfus. Harry brought this fellow to Chicago and spent a week talking to him at $300 a day. June Martino was afraid I was going to blow my top and throw Harry and his consultant both into the street. But that was the farthest thing from my mind. I know that you have to spend money to make money, and as far as I was concerned, Harry was simply doing the job I'd hired him to do.

One of the reasons his subordinated lease idea worked so well was that in the late fifties we didn't have the proliferation of franchise operations and the fierce competition for commercial fringe property that developed in the course of the next twenty years. Another reason was that both Harry and I were pretty good salesmen, and we could romance a property owner with the notion of earning at least a little something from his vacant land.

This was the beginning of real income for McDonald's. Harry devised a formula for the monthly payments being made by our operators that paid our own mortgage and other expenses plus a profit. We received this set monthly minimum or a percentage of the volume the operator did, whichever was greater. After a time we began realizing substantial revenues from the formula, and we could see that we were merely nibbling around the edges of this huge hamburger frontier we were exploring.

I recall that Harry made a trip out to San Bernardino about the time we were really starting to roll, and Dick McDonald asked him what he thought the future of McDonald's would be. Harry told him that one day this company would be bigger than F. W. Woolworth. Dick really did a double take at that. He told me later, "I thought you had a genuine nut on your hands, Ray." But Harry knew exactly where he wanted to go, and he knew how to get there.

In one of the impromptu meetings that Harry, June, and I frequently had after hours in the office, or in my home, Harry said, "We are doing fine with these bank mortgages, but if we are to gain any stature in the financial community, we are going to have to get some big institutional investors to back us." I agreed, and Harry went after the insurance companies. The first deal he made was with All-American Life Insurance Company in Chicago. They agreed to arrange a number of mortgages for us. Then he succeeded in lining up Central Standard Life, also in Chicago.

This was great news. We were moving ahead, gathering momentum; we could see the day that we would start making a profit. I felt deeply indebted to Harry and June. They worked tirelessly, and I knew that both of them were neglecting their family obligations completely so that they could stay on top of things in our rapidly building operation. June later told me that all the while her two boys were growing up, she never made it to one of their birthday parties or graduation ceremonies, and there were several times that she had to be in the office on Christmas. I knew what she and Harry were doing, because I was in the same boat. It was a little easier for me, perhaps, because of the continuing cold war between Ethel, my daughter, and me. My total commitment to business had long since been established in my home. But that made me feel all the more grateful toward Harry and June. I couldn't give them raises to compensate them for their past efforts, but I could make sure that they would be rewarded when McDonald's became one of the country's major companies, which I never doubted it would. I gave them stock—ten percent to June and twenty percent to Harry—and ultimately it would make them rich. At the time, of course, Chicago Transit Authority tokens would have been worth more.

Every once in a while when I walked past Harry's office, I would ask, "By the way, Harry, what do you hear from Clem Bohr?"

"Just had a phone call from him the other day," Harry would say. "He seems to be cooking with gas. He's got a location in Cleveland that he'll start building on any day now." Next Bohr got a site in Wisconsin, and then we had reports that he'd acquired two pieces of property in downstate Illinois. Each time I got one of these bulletins, I'd say, "Cripes, that's great, Harry; wonderful," and we'd talk about what a terrific guy Clem Bohr was.

Cooking with gas was a popular expression at the time, but it was an in-joke with us. When somebody was *cooking with gas* around our place it meant that he was really doing everything right. This stemmed from our experience in patterning our stores on the plans provided by the McDonald brothers. Jim Schindler insisted on using gas units for making french fries instead of the electric friers the McDonald boys were using. Gas proved to be more efficient for this purpose. It was cheaper, and we got a better product. So we tried to "cook with gas" in all our operations at McDonald's.

The experience with the Waukegan store and the others we opened during the summer and fall of 1956 brought home to me the fact that I needed a good operations man in corporate headquarters. I was committed in each franchise agreement to furnish the licensee with experienced help to train his crew and get the McDonald's system working in his store. I couldn't afford to bring Art Bender from California each time, and I couldn't spare Ed MacLuckie from the Des Plaines store very often, so I had to give some of the operators a $100 discount in lieu of the promised assistance. This was not good at all, because insistence on quality has to be emphasized in every procedure, and every crew member must be drilled in the McDonald's method of providing service. These basic elements will insure success for a store, unless its location is unspeakably bad, and we have had only a few instances of that in more than twenty years. But the fundamentals do not spring forth, self-evident and active, from the brow of every former grocery clerk, soda jerk, military man, or specialist in one of the hundreds of other callings who join the ranks of McDonald's operators. Quite the contrary; the basics have to be stressed over and over. If I had a brick for every time I've repeated the phrase *QSC and V* (Quality, Service, Cleanliness, and Value), I think I'd probably be able to bridge the Atlantic Ocean with them.   And the operators need the stress on fundamentals as much as their managers and crews.   This is especially true of a new location.

So I needed someone to handle operations.   Harry and June agreed, but since they didn't come into contact with the day-to-day routine in stores as I did, they were at a loss for suggestions. "God, you'd need a real dynamo, Ray," said June Martino.   "You haven't got anybody with the experience of an Art Bender or an Ed MacLuckie.   Who could you get?"

"Never mind," I assured her.   "I think I know just the guy."

8

Fred Turner.

That was the name I had in mind for the position of corporate operations man. I have a mental snapshot on file that shows Fred, who one day would become President and then Chairman of the Board of McDonald's, as he looked when he first walked into my office, in February 1956. He was little more than a kid, twenty-three years old. He had a baby face and the most infectious grin I'd seen in years. He and another young fellow named Joe Post came in to answer an ad I had run in the *Chicago Tribune* for franchisees. Fred and Joe and two other members of their families had formed what they called the Post-Turner Corporation. Their aim was to buy a McDonald's franchise, which Fred and Joe would operate. I gladly took their down payment on the license fee and suggested that it would be a good thing if they learned the ropes by working in the Des Plaines store while waiting to get their own location going. Fred took me up on it. He went to work immediately for $1 an hour. He was also getting $85 a week from his family group, an advance they agreed to consider part of the cost of getting into the business, although Fred was obligated to pay it back eventually.

Fred was a terrific worker. He had a natural feel for the rhythms and priorities that make a McDonald's restaurant click. This talent quickly showed up in the reports I got from Ed MacLuckie. Even Art Jacobs, who spent very little time around the store, noticed Fred. I could see he was a born leader, and I was happy that he was going to be one of my franchisees. At least I thought he was until the Post-Turner Corporation began having problems. One of their basic rules was that the decision on where their franchise was to be located had to be unanimous. They could get two votes on a number of sites, and, occasionally, three. But never could all four agree.

I gathered that Fred was getting pretty disgusted with the situation. After a time he quit accepting the family group's subsidy and took a second job selling Fuller Brushes. He was afraid they never would find a location, and he didn't want to go deeply in debt to the enterprise. Late in the fall of 1956, Bill Barr, operator of a newly opened store on Cicero Avenue in Chicago, asked if he could have Fred as his manager.

"Yes, you can," I told him. "But remember that I want him in the corporation. When the time comes, I am going to take him."

The time came sooner than I anticipated. We had a difficult situation developing down in Kankakee, Illinois, with one of the pieces of property we were acquiring for Franchise Realty. We needed an operator there, so I sent Harry Sonneborn around to talk to Fred to see if he would take that store and run it for us. He agreed, but then the deal fell through, and I asked him to come to work downtown instead.

"I'll pay you $425 a month," I said, and he brightened at that. Then he did some fast mental arithmetic and figured that it was the same as the $100 a week he was getting at the Cicero Avenue store.

"I can't really do it for that, Mr. Kroc," he said. "I'd be losing, because I'd be getting the same pay, but it would cost me more to travel to the Loop; I'd have to buy lunches, which I don't have to do at the store, and I'd have to wear a suit all the time and pay for cleaning and having white shirts laundered. No. I couldn't do it for less than $475 a month.

"You're right," I said. "Four seventy-five it is." He brightened up again, and we shook on it. That was the last conversation I ever had with Fred Turner about his salary.

Fred came to work in our office in January 1957, a year in which we opened twenty-five new McDonald's operations around the country. He was in on all of them. So were Jim Schindler, our stainless-steel magician from Leitner Equipment Company, and Syg Chakow, the salesman from Illinois Range. Both Jim and Syg worked as if they were on my payroll. They put in many hours of overtime making sure the equipment was right and seeing that it was installed properly. Sometimes they even helped clean up scrap lumber and sweep the parking lot to help a licensee meet his opening deadline. In Sarasota, Florida, they ran into a health department ruling that deemed it unsanitary to prepare milk shakes and hamburgers in the same room. In our units, of course, the shakes were made close by the griddles, and it would have been prohibitively expensive to redesign our structure. Syg Chakow came up with the idea of building a glass partition with an inside door so that the shakes and hamburgers could be prepared in separate rooms, yet served to customers through a single window. The health department was satisfied, and our operator was greatly relieved.

Harry, June, and I were talking about the Sarasota saga one midnight near the end of 1957. We were sitting in the recreation room of my home in Arlington Heights after one of our brain-wringing strategy conferences, and the subject was all the close shaves we'd had in getting units open. We were feeling kind of giddy with the accomplishment of having thirty-seven McDonald's hamburger restaurants in operation and the prospect of doing much better in the coming year. I told them there'd always been problems with openings, beginning with the McDonald brothers' first self-service store in 1948. Now San Bernardino is on the edge of the desert, remember, and you could probably put its average annual precipitation in a martini glass and still have room for an olive. But on the day the McDonald boys opened their new drive-in, it snowed three inches in San Bernardino! What few customers did make it through the traffic jams and into their parking lot sat in their cars and honked their horns angrily. Snow had covered the signs that advertised self service—no carhops.

An equally unusual thing happened in 1953 when the McDonalds were designing their "golden arches" building. They wanted to lay it out in the most efficient way possible, placing windows and equipment so that each crew member's job could be done with a minimum number of steps. Mac and Dick had a tennis court behind their house, and they got Art Bender and a couple of other operations people up there to draw out the whole floor plan with chalk, actual size, like a giant hopscotch. It must have looked funny as hell—those grown men pacing about and going through the motions of preparing hamburgers, french fries, and milk shakes. Anyhow, they got it all drawn, just so, and the architect was to come up the next day and copy the layout to scale for his plans. That night there was a terrific rainstorm in San Bernardino, and every chalk mark on that tennis court was washed away.

"What did they do, go through the whole damned procedure again?" Harry asked.

"Oh, sure," I replied. "That's how they came up with the design Jim Schindler adapted for us."

"Listen, Ray," June cut in, "I think you ought to hire Jim. You're going to need him."

June's suggestion made a lot of sense, and we did hire Jim Schindler, our second employee in the corporate office. I had to pay him $12,000 a year, which was more than Harry, June, or I were getting, but we badly needed his expertise. I don't think he would have come with us for that salary if I weren't Bohemian like him. He trusted me, and the association worked well. The suggestion that we hire him was a credit to June. But I was surprised by the directness of her statement. Usually June would drop hints here and there and try to transfer her enthusiasm to Harry and me by womanly wiles. This always amused me. June set great store by her "feminine intuition." Some people actually thought she was psychic. But I didn't need a horoscope to tell me the value of her role in our office. She acted as a buffer between two pile-driving personalities, Harry Sonneborn's and mine, and most of the time she succeeded in keeping us from colliding head-on. Clashes were inevitable, though, because while Harry and I shared a belief in the capitalistic system and while we had the same faith in our enterprise and its future, our individual approaches were quite different.

Harry was the scholarly type. He analyzed situations on the

My father looks serious in my favorite photograph of him, but there's a hint of a mischievous smile ready to spread across his face. He loved to laugh and sing. He worried himself to death, however, over his losses in the Depression.

My little brother, Bob, and I pose with mother in the yard of our Oak Park home.

In our Sunday best, Bob, Lorraine, and I strike an "Our Gang" pose on the steps of our old back porch. The misty eye of baseball memory recalls the Lincoln grammar school team below as a pretty formidable nine. The boy who would one day become the owner of the San Diego Padres is standing third from the left in the top row.

One of my early business ventures was the Ray Kroc Music Emporium, which I opened in 1916. I was the "piano man," playing sheet music my partners and I were trying to sell. It was fun while it lasted. When World War I was declared, I was eager to become an ambulance driver for the Red Cross. In the photo below I was all set to ship out to France. Happily, however, the war ended before my departure.

As a salesman of ladies' notions, I believed in being a snappy dresser. White socks and pointed shoes polished to mirror brightness were the rage.

June Martino . . . a brilliant waif.   Dick McDonald . . . fast-food pioneer.

Harry Sonneborn . . . financial wizard.

Fred Turner . . . griddle man extraordinary.

The original McDonald brothers' store in San Bernardino, California (left), was an octagonal hamburger factory that kept eight Multimixers busy. This phenomenon is what attracted me and led to my deal with the McDonald boys. Above is the architect's rendering of the original Golden Arches installation, which replaced the octagonal building.

Number one—my Des Plaines store, opened in June 1955 with a flock of afflictions, most of them due to difficulties of adapting a near-desert-style structure to a cold climate. It was not in the greatest location, but it made a profit from the outset and set a pattern for other stores.

That's me with the hose washing down in front of the store. I may have been the owner, but I wasn't too proud to clean up. That's still true.

Our fifth anniversary was a big event for me, June Martino, and Harry Sonneborn. We now had 200 restaurants and annual sales of $37 million.

Here's a typical contract between me and Lou Perlman, McDonald's original paper supplier. A handshake was all we ever needed to bind an agreement.

I never became a top banana in show business, but a company did name me top pickle. Things were never dull in our headquarters in the early years.

This was the McDonald's gang at our first office Christmas party in 1958. From left to right, they are: (front row) John Horn, Lillian McMahon, Sue Steinbach, Helen Shelby, Ray Czerwinski. (Second row) Gertrude Jacobs, Elaine Bush, Nancy Jenkins, Karen Moore. (Third row) Gloria Burr, Hazel Striepling, Mary Ann Summins, Ray Kroc, June Martino, Harry Sonneborn, Idamae Case, Dorothy Brown, and Trudel Molitor. (Fourth row) Don Conley, Tony Felker, John Rice, Alex Pukalo, Nick Karos, Tom Casey, Miriam Cain, Richard Boylan, Robert Livett. (Fifth row) Fred Turner, Barry Freed, Ralph Bauwens, James Schindler, Robert Papp, Kenneth Whitton, and John Haran. It was a happy group that was truly green and growing.

A graduating class from Hamburger U. greet Fred Turner and me after receiving their diplomas. The school opened in basement of the Elk Grove store in 1961.

Two symbols of the Sixties: President John F. Kennedy smiling as he mingles with a crowd, and another bright new McDonald's store opening. Left: Norman Rockwell made the McDonald's All-American image official by painting a young crew member serving a crowd of happy kids. Original hangs in the headquarters of McDonald's in Oak Brook, Ill.

Operations imitation—that's Fred Turner serving me fries at a meeting. Kidding aside, McDonald's executives have first-hand operations know-how.

Operations in action—a view from behind the counter at a new McDonald's hamburger restaurant in the Woodfield shopping center in suburban Chicago.

Operations analysis—a typical classroom scene at Hamburger U. Nowhere is the business of food service studied more seriously or scientifically.

Joni, the ideal partner in music and marriage.

Our red-and-white tile buildings became landmarks across the U. S., but we eventually outgrew them. . . . Fred Turner and I pushed hard to develop the new brick buildings with their mansard roofs and indoor seating. It was exciting each time we went over plans for a new one. . . . The photo below shows a typical McDonald's of the '70s. Now, as the photos at the bottom of the page indicate, our building plans extend around the world.

Joni and I join our schnauzer, Burgomeister, in a big smile for a friend's snapshot. At left—"Our Gang" grown older—Bob, Lorraine, and I in front of the Kroc Foundation headquarters. Below: The McDonald's board of directors in a portrait taken in February 1977. Seated, from left, Fred Turner, Ray Kroc, Ed Schmitt, and Dick Boylan; standing, Allen Stults, chairman of the board of American National Bank & Trust Co., Dave Wallerstein, business consultant and former president of the Balaban & Katz movie theater chain, Don Lubin, Bob Thurston, senior vice-president of Quaker Oats Co., and Gerry Newman.

Entertainer Danny Thomas joined me in celebrating my gift to St. Jude's Children's Hospital, part of the $7.5 million I gave on my 70th birthday.

Buzzy Bavasi, who bosses the San Diego Padres, with their owner and chief fan.

Art Bender, my first franchisee, shows his readiness to go to bat for me again.

Ronald McDonald leads a parade of great promotions that conveyed our message...

... Like the teenager's T-shirt slogan, they became part of the American scene.

Dr. Norman Vincent Peale presents me with the Horatio Alger award, one of my most cherished honors.

Below: Padres' new owner acknowledges fans' cheers . . . prelude to tirade that made baseball history.

Next to baseball, my favorite occupation outside McDonald's is the business of The Kroc Foundation. Members of its board of directors meeting below are: (from left) Mrs. Robert (Alice) Kroc, Harry H. Haggey, Jr., Fred Turner, Al Doty, Robert Kroc, Anthony G. Zulfer, Jr., Mrs. Ray (Joan) Kroc, Ray A. Kroc, and Don Lubin. Haggey and Zulfer are investment advisers for the Foundation.

basis of management theory and economic principles. I proceeded on the strength of my salesman's instinct and my subjective assessment of people. I have often been asked to explain the methods I use in choosing executives, because much of the success of my organization has been a result of the kind of people I have picked for key positions. My answers aren't very satisfying; they don't sound much different than the rules that students of business administration find in their basic textbooks. It's hard to come up with real answers because the weight of the judgment is not in the rule but in the application. As a result, I have sometimes been accused of being arbitrary. June Martino believed, for example, that I once fired a member of our staff because he didn't wear the right kind of hat and didn't keep his shoes shined. She was correct as far as it went, I *didn't* like those things about the man, but those weren't the reasons I fired him. I just knew that he wasn't right for us; he was prone to making mistakes, and the hat and the shoes were merely symptoms of his sloppy way of thinking.

I've been wrong in my judgments about men, I suppose, but not very often. Bob Frost, one of our key executives on the West Coast, will remember the time he and I were checking out stores, and I got a very unfavorable impression of one of his young managers. As we drove away from the store I said to Bob, "I think you'd better fire that man."

"Oh, Ray, come on!" he exclaimed. "Give the kid a break. He's young, he has a good attitude, and I think he will come along."

"You could be right, Bob," I said, "but I don't think so. He has no potential."

Later in the day, as we were driving back to Los Angeles, that conversation was still bugging me. Finally I turned to Bob and yelled, "Listen goddammit, I want you to fire that man!"

One thing that makes Bob Frost a good executive is that he has the courage of his convictions. He also sticks up for his people. He's a retired Navy man, and he knows how to keep his head under fire. He simply pursed his lips and nodded solemnly and said, "If you are ordering me to do it, Ray, I will. But I would like to give him another six months and see how he works out."

I agreed, reluctantly. What happened after that was the kind of personnel hocus-pocus that government is famous for but should never be permitted in business, least of all in McDonald's. The man hung on. He was on the verge of being fired several times in the following years, but he was transferred or got a new supervisor each time. He was a decent guy, so each new boss would struggle to reform him. Many years later he was fired. The assessment of the executive who finally swung the ax was that "this man has no potential."

Bob Frost now admits he was wrong. I had the guy pegged accurately from the outset. But that's not the point. Our expenditure of time and effort on that fellow was wasted and, worst of all, he spent several years of his life in what turned out to be a blind alley. It would have been far better for his career if he'd been severed early and forced to find work more suited to his talents. It was an unfortunate episode for both parties, but it serves to show that an astute judgment can seem arbitrary to everyone but the man who makes it.

My executive style was prone to that sort of thing far more than Harry Sonneborn's. On the other hand, his cool, dispassionate manner didn't inspire much spirit and enthusiasm. I like to get people fired up, fill them with zeal for McDonald's, and watch the results in their work.

We were different, Harry and I, but for a long time we were able to splice our efforts so that the differences made us stronger. Fred Turner added another dimension to the combination. It became part of Fred's assignment in helping new operators to open their stores to deal with the local suppliers of meat, buns, and condiments, and this exposure, combined with his experience at the griddle, helped us make significant changes in the way things were supplied to us and how they were packaged.

Consider, for example, the hamburger bun. It requires a certain kind of mind to see beauty in a hamburger bun. Yet, is it any more unusual to find grace in the texture and softly curved silhouette of a bun than to reflect lovingly on the hackles of a favorite fishing fly? Or the arrangement of textures and colors in a butterfly's wing? Not if you are a McDonald's man. Not if you view the bun as an essential material in the art of serving a great many meals fast. Then this plump yeasty mass becomes an object worthy of sober study. Fred Turner gave the bun that sort of attention. We were buying our buns in the midwest from Louis Kuchuris' Mary Ann Bakery. At first they were cluster buns, meaning that the buns were attached to each other in clusters of four to six, and they were only partially sliced. Fred pointed out that it would be much easier and faster for a griddle man if we had individual buns instead of clusters and if they were sliced all the way through. The baker could afford to do it our way because of the large quantities of buns we were ordering. Fred also worked with a cardboard box manufacturer on the design of a sturdy, reusable box for our buns. Handling these boxes instead of the customary packages of twelve reduced the baker's packaging cost, so he was able to give us a better price on the buns. It also reduced our shipping costs and streamlined our operations. With the old packages, it didn't take long for a busy griddle man to find himself buried in paper. Then there was the time spent opening packages, pulling buns from the cluster, and halving them. These fractions of seconds added up to wasted minutes. A well-run restaurant is like a winning baseball team, it makes the most of every crew member's talent and takes advantage of every split-second opportunity to speed up service. Once our bun box was in use, Fred kept coming up with little refinements on it. He found that buns would stay moister longer in the box if the lid came all the way down to the bottom instead of halfway. He also learned that the number of reuses we could get from a box was increased if he had an extra heavy coating of wax applied by the maker.

So Fred would go out to Milwaukee or Moline or Kalamazoo or wherever a new operation was starting, and he'd call on a baker there and tell him about McDonald's and the buns we would like him to make for us. Fred had the figures laid out cold, so the baker could see why our way was better and how it would save him money. He'd never heard of the kind of box we wanted, usually, so Fred would set up a meeting with the box manufacturer.

Supplying buns to McDonald's was the break of a lifetime for many of these men. Mary Ann Bakery, for example, was a small organization when it started dealing with us. Now it has a plant with a quarter-mile-long conveyor belt for cooling buns after they're baked. The firm uses more than a million pounds of flour a month to make buns for us. Mary Ann also has a trucking company that services many McDonald's. Freund Baking, now a division of CFS Continental, is another company that grew with us. I had to twist Harold Freund's arm repeatedly to get him to build a bakery just to service our California stores. Freund now has the largest, most automated bun plant in the world. It produces eight thousand buns an hour for McDonald's. It also has a plant in St. Petersburg serving all of Florida, and another serving all of Hawaii.

Fred applied the same sort of thinking he'd used on buns to all the other supplies being purchased. It's important to make clear here that Fred wasn't buying these items on behalf of the corporation, and we weren't selling to the operators. We set the standards for quality and recommended methods for packaging, but the operators themselves did the purchasing from suppliers. Our stores were selling only nine items, and they were buying only thirty-five or forty items with which to make the nine. So although a McDonald's restaurant's purchasing power was no greater in total than that of any other restaurant in a given area, it was concentrated. A McDonald's bought more buns, more catsup, more mustard, and so forth, and this gave it a terrific position in the marketplace for those items. We enhanced that position by figuring out ways a supplier could lower his costs, which meant, of course, that he could afford to sell to a McDonald's for less. Bulk packaging was one way; another was making it possible for him to deliver more items per stop.

A side benefit of the purchasing system we were working out as we went along was that it gave us an automatic inventory check. An operator could balance off the number of buns used in a day against the number of patties used, and if they didn't come out even, something was wrong. He could keep a close check on waste, and he could spot pilferage almost immediately. If he was supposed to be getting ten patties of meat to a pound, he'd know something was wrong if he went through 110 pounds of meat in serving a number of buns that should have used only 100 pounds. Either his meat man was shorting him or someone was stealing it.

Whenever Fred came up with a better idea of handling a product, I'd see to it that our suppliers implemented it in all their operations. My years of experience in selling paper cups and Multimixers paid off here, because I knew exactly what hands held the strings I wanted to pull to get the job done. People have marveled at the fact that I didn't start McDonald's until I was fifty-two years old, and then I became a success overnight. But I was just like a lot of show business personalities who work away quietly at their craft for years, and then, suddenly, they get the right break and make it big. I was an overnight success all right, but thirty years is a long, long night.

I always felt comfortable working with Fred Turner, because he is a detail man like I am. There is a certain kind of mind that conceives new ideas as complete systems with all of their parts functioning. I don't think in that "grand design" pattern. I work from the part to the whole, and I don't move on to the large scale ideas until I have perfected the small details. To me this is a much more flexible approach. For example, when I was starting McDonald's, my original purpose was to sell more Multimixers. If I had fixed that in my mind as a master plan and worked unswervingly toward that end, my system would have been a far different and much smaller-scale creation. Once in a while I have had great ideas strike me in the middle of the night—sweeping plans that I could see complete, or so it seemed. But, every time, these things turned out in the clear light of the following day to be more fanciful than functional. And the reason usually was that some small but essential detail had been overlooked in my grand design. So, at the risk of seeming simplistic, I emphasize the importance of details. You must perfect every fundamental of your business if you expect it to perform well.

We demonstrated this emphasis on details, and saw it pay off, in our approach to hamburger patties. Now a hamburger patty is a piece of meat. But a McDonald's hamburger patty is a piece of meat with character. The first thing that distinguishes it from the patties that many other places pass off as hamburgers is that it is all beef. There are no hearts or other alien goodies ground into our patties. The fat content of our patty is a prescribed nineteen percent and it is rigidly controlled. There is much that could be written on the technical history of the McDonald's hamburger patty, the experiments with different grinding methods, freezing techniques, and surface conformations in order to arrive at the juiciest and most flavorful piece of meat we could produce for our system. But, fascinating as it is, that's another story.

I first became aware of the hamburger patty as an element of food purveying when I was a young man going to dances on Chicago's West Side. There was a White Castle on the corner of Ogden and Harlem Avenues, where we could go for hamburgers after a dance. They used a sort of tiny ice cream scoop to make a patty about one-inch square, and they sold their burgers by the bagful. Then, at the World's Fair in 1933, Swift & Company had all the concessions, and they introduced frozen blocks of ground beef that had five holes concealed in them. The holes allowed the concession operator to get two more patties to the block—eighteen instead of sixteen. It is possible, of course, to make money by employing such material-stretching methods. One time a McDonald's operator came to me with the idea he'd dreamed up to cut costs by producing a doughnut-shaped patty. His notion was to plug the hole with condiments, and cover it with a pickle so the customer wouldn't notice the hole. I told him we wanted to feed our customers, not fleece them, but I couldn't suppress a chuckle at the outrageous con artistry of the idea; a real Chicago fast one.

We decided that our patties would be ten to the pound, and that soon became the standard for the industry. Fred did a lot of experimenting in the packaging of patties, too. There was a kind of paper that was exactly right, he felt, and he tested and tested until he found out what it was. It had to have enough wax on it so that the patty would pop off without sticking when you slapped it onto the griddle. But it couldn't be too stiff or the patties would slide and refuse to stack up. There also was a science in stacking patties. If you made the stack too high, the ones on the bottom would be misshapen and dried out. So we arrived at the optimum stack, and that determined the height of our meat suppliers' packages. The purpose of all these refinements, and we never lost sight of it, was to make our griddle man's job easier to do quickly and well. All the other considerations of cost cutting, inventory control, and so forth were important to be sure, but they were secondary to the critical detail of what happened there at that smoking griddle. This was the vital passage in our assembly line, and the product had to flow through it smoothly or the whole plant would falter.

By the end of his first year in our office, Fred Turner had pretty much taken over the purchasing for us. Another thing he'd done in weeks when there were no stores opening was to visit existing stores and chat with the operators. He went down to Urbana first, then up to Waukegan, spending a day in each store. When he came back he gave me a little checklist he'd devised to show how these operations were doing. That list evolved into the format for our field consultations, which today is a vital part of our system-wide quality assurance.

I've sometimes wondered what would have happened if the Post-Turner Corporation had found a site all four partners could agree on and Fred had become an operator. I'm sure he would have done extremely well, just as other members of the group did: Joe Post, for example, is an operator in Springfield, Missouri. He and his wife have three stores, including one on the city's new Battlefield Mall that has five dining rooms on different levels, with fireplaces and fine paintings. It's a veritable Taj Mahal among McDonald's restaurants. Fred would have carved out an empire for himself no matter where he'd gone. I am sure of that, not only because I know him but because I know his wife. Patty Turner has allowed her husband to be successful. I know that she would have been right in there pitching with him if he'd chosen to become an operator. Since a McDonald's restaurant is a prime example of American small business in action, the husband-wife team is basic for us. Typically, the husband will look after operations and maintenance while his wife keeps the books and handles personnel. This mutual interest extends into all levels of the company, and I've always encouraged corporate executive wives to get involved in their husbands' work—two heads are better than one, whether a guy is manning a griddle and sweating out getting started in his own store or shuffling papers behind a fancy desk.

9

I knew something was drastically wrong as soon as I heard the tone of June Martino's voice on the telephone. She said Harry Sonneborn had to talk to me immediately. I felt a queasy foreboding that this problem would have something to do with Clem Bohr. Harry and I had discussed Bohr and his recent strange behavior just before I'd left Chicago to look over some new locations on the East Coast.

Bohr now had eight sites on which he had McDonald's buildings in various stages of completion. He'd been giving us enthusiastic reports all along, but suddenly he'd grown remote and uncommunicative. He didn't return Harry's calls, and June had been trying to reach him for a couple of weeks without success.

Harry came on the line from our attorney's office. "Ray," he said, "I'm afraid we are in deep trouble."

"Don't tell me . . . is it Clem Bohr?" I asked.

"You guessed it. We have had mechanic's liens filed against us on the locations he's leased to us. The son of a bitch never got clear title to any of this property. He never had the things financed. Now the owners are coming back on us."

My reply to that probably melted a few miles of Bell System's wires. Suddenly our little company's promise of prosperity looked more like the brink of bankruptcy. "What the hell are we going to do, Harry?" I shouted. "How much money are we talking about?"

"Well, Ray, it's going to be at least $400,000," he said.

"Jesus!"

"Ray, I have an idea that I think could pull us out of this," he said. "We can ask for a loan from our McDonald's suppliers, I figure $300,000. Then I know a fellow in Peoria named Harry Blanchard. He married a widow who owns a big brewery, and he has some money to lend. I think he'll help us out."

It made sense to me. If anyone stood to gain by our success and suffer if we failed, it was our suppliers. They knew McDonald's restaurants possessed the potential of becoming super customers, and they knew we played straight. So I told Harry, by God, to go full speed ahead with it. He did, and it worked like a charm. Lou Perlman of Perlman Paper Company (later to become the Martin-Brower Corporation), Les Karlstedt of the Elgin Dairy Company, Louis Kuchuris of Mary Ann Baking Company, and Al Cohn of CFS Continental all agreed to make loans. Harry's friend Blanchard and his associate, Carl Young, also lent us money.

I don't remember what happened to Clem Bohr. It seems to me that he went into the hamburger business in competition with us and lost his shirt. That happened to a number of sharpies who tried to spin off an operation they'd started with us in order to build a personal empire. Bohr probably would have done very well if he'd stuck by his original agreement and been less greedy. The situation he forced us into is a good example of how adversity can strengthen you if you have the will to grind it out. It put us in a precarious financial condition, but we were eight fine locations to the good, and the spirit of mutual support it fostered with our suppliers would be very beneficial in the future. Perhaps the most positive result of the Bohr fiasco, however, was that it gave us courage to borrow heavily so we could expand McDonald's more rapidly.

My net worth in 1959 was about $90,000. This made it rather difficult to borrow money in the big amounts that Harry and I had in mind. I recall asking David Kennedy, chairman of the board of Continental Illinois National Bank of Chicago, for a loan. The man who would later become Secretary of the Treasury under Richard Nixon listened politely to my sales pitch on McDonald's vitality and growth potential. Then he asked to see my balance sheet. After glancing over the single page, he stood up, and I knew the interview was over. He was kind about it, and I suppose I really couldn't blame him. Yet I resented the rebuff, and you can be sure that I did my banking elsewhere from then on.

About this same time, Harry had been approached by an insurance salesman named Milton Goldstandt, who said he could arrange financing for us with the John Hancock Life Insurance Company. He wanted a pretty hefty fee for arranging the deal, plus a certain portion of our stock, and I was opposed to this. But Harry wanted to pursue it anyhow and see where it led.

First thing I knew, Goldstandt had brought in an older gentleman named Lee Stack, who had been a financial vice-president of the John Hancock Company and had retired to become a limited partner with Paine, Webber, Jackson & Curtis, the stockbrokers. Harry Sonneborn and Lee Stack began flying all over the damned country cooking up financial deals for McDonald's. As it turned out, I didn't have to worry about giving any stock to Goldstandt, because the big loan arrangement with the Hancock didn't work out. However, with Stack's help, Harry arranged more than a dozen mortgages with the John Hancock.

Somewhere in the course of our loan discussions, the idea emerged that we should build and operate ten or so stores as a company. This would give us a firm base of income in the event the McDonald brothers claimed default on our contract (I had yet to receive a single registered letter from them authorizing our buildings to be constructed with basements and furnaces). If worse came to worst, the thinking went, we could always retrench and operate our company stores under some other name. The germ of this idea, too, might have sprung from our dealings with Clem Bohr, in which case I thank him in the same spirit one thanks the robber who at least spared his life.

Establishing company stores, of course, would require a truly massive infusion of capital. But Harry said he thought he could arrange it with the help of his friend Lee Stack.

The proposition that Harry finally brought to me was for three

insurance companies to lend us $1.5 million in exchange for about
22½ percent of our stock. Harry introduced me to Fred Fideli,
who represented State Mutual Life Assurance, and John Gosnell
of the Paul Revere Life Insurance Company. These two men
explained how they had arranged with their firms and the
Massachusetts Protective Association to make the loan. I was
intrigued by the proposal, and I was impressed with Fideli and
Gosnell. The only problem seemed to be how we would handle
the deal among ourselves. My Bohemian frugality fought with the
idea of giving up any part of the stock in the company I had
struggled so desperately to build; yet the appeal of $1.5 million
was irresistible. The arrangement we came up with, after a lot of
discussion, was that I would contribute 22½ percent of my
remaining stock (leaving me with 54¼ percent), Harry would put
in 22½ percent and June Martino would give up 22½ percent of
hers.

It turned out to be the best deal those three insurance companies ever made. They sold their stock a few years later for
between $7 and $10 million. That is one hell of a return on
investment. (However, if they'd waited until 1973 to sell, they
could have gotten over five hundred million dollars!)

That loan could be called the lift-off stage of McDonald's
rocketlike growth in the sixties. It took a lot more financial thrust
to put us into orbit, but we would never have gotten off the ground
without it. Our first McOpCo (McDonald's Operating Company)
store was purchased from an operator in Torrence, California. A
short time later, in the summer of 1960, we opened our first
company-built store in Columbus, Ohio.

I took my hat off to Harry Sonneborn then for negotiating that
loan, and I still do today. Yet the results of it, in terms of the
posture Harry was giving the company, contained the seeds of a
philosophical clash that eventually would split Harry and me and
nearly destroy McDonald's. It was then that Harry's view of the
corporation as just a real estate business, rather than a hamburger
business, began to crystalize. As he had set it up, we would not
take a mortgage for more than ten years, even on a subordinated
basis. We had twenty-year leases on all the property. This meant,
of course, that after ten years when our mortgages were paid off,

we would have all the income from a store free and clear to the corporation. That was fine. But Harry's line of thought had this annex: Since we were not obliged to renew licenses, at the expiration of the licenses the company could wind up operating all of the stores. I would not agree with that. I never did and I never will. It can't happen so long as my influence and that of Fred Turner enforce the view that the corporation is in the hamburger restaurant business, and its vitality depends on the energy of many individual owner-operators. The corporation has purchased stores—many of them, as I will show in later chapters. But our procedures for doing so are clearly spelled out to franchisees. We bend over backward to be fair in every case. We recognize that it would be unwieldy and counterproductive for the corporation to own more than about thirty percent of all stores. Our slogan for McDonald's operators is "In business for yourself, but not by yourself," and it is one of the secrets of our success.

A curious circumstance developed for the company in the momentum generated by the loan from the three insurance companies. We could show that we were making a profit now. At the same time, we had no cash flow.

The reason for this was simply that the accounting regulations were weak in the area of deferred expenses you could carry on your books. We were capitalizing all the real estate overhead and all the construction overhead for a period of eighteen months. We called this "Developmental Accounting," and it allowed us to show a bottom line profit. But it was distorting our profit and loss statements.

We hired a regular parade of people in the late fifties. We sold them a dream and paid them as little as possible. I don't feel bad about that, because I wasn't making much myself, and those who stayed with us are now very well off, indeed.

Bob Papp was hired as a draftsman to assist Jim Schindler. He later became a vice-president in charge of construction. John Haran came into the company to help Harry with real estate. These added people meant that we needed more space, of course, so we kept moving around in the area where I had had my original two-room office, knocking down walls and expanding.

One day Harry came in and told me he was going to hire a

young fellow named Dick Boylan to help him with finances. "He's a lawyer and accountant, and he's our kind of guy, Ray," Harry said. "Let me tell you what he did. He and his partner, whose name is Bob Ryan, are selling insurance, see? They know they have about as much chance as a snowball in hell of getting to see me with that act. But it happens that they both used to work for the Internal Revenue Service, so they tell my secretary they are from the IRS. Naturally, I think, 'Holy Christ, what now?' And I call June in to listen to what they have to say. Boylan gives me this kind of sheepish grin and says, 'With our background of working for the IRS, Mr. Sonneborn, we know we can design an insurance plan that will help you. . . .' Well, that breaks June up, and I have a hard time keeping a straight face myself.

"Their insurance proposal was pretty good, too. It was a hell of a presentation. June was very impressed, and she's the one who suggested hiring him."

Dick Boylan is now senior executive vice-president and chief financial officer of the company. Some time after he joined us we also hired his former partner, Bob Ryan, and he's a vice-president and treasurer. I could go on and on listing people who joined us at this time, many of whom are now officers of McDonald's or wealthy operators. One of our fine old-timers, Morris Goldfarb from Los Angeles, said at the 1976 operator's convention in Hawaii that he was certain research would show that Ray Kroc has made millionaires of more men than any other person in history. I don't know about that; I appreciate Morrie's view, but I would put it another way. I'd rather say I gave a lot of men the opportunity to become millionaires. They did it themselves. I merely provided the means. But I certainly do know a powerful number of success stories.

McDonald's doesn't confer success on anyone. It takes guts and staying power to make it with one of our restaurants. At the same time, it doesn't require any unusual aptitude or intellect. Any man with common sense, dedication to principles, and a love of hard work can do it. And I have stood flatfooted before big crowds of our operators and asserted that any man who gets a McDonald's store today and works at it relentlessly will become a success, and many will become millionaires—no question.

There are hazards and pitfalls, of course, just as there are in any small business. And some locations go along for years with a very modest volume. But, almost without exception, these stores will catch on at some point and begin to grow, as Morrie Goldfarb himself can testify. He was one of my very first franchisees. His store on La Tijera Boulevard in Los Angeles opened a year after my place in Des Plaines. I went out to look at his location, and it was excellent. I congratulated him on it. But for some reason it turned out to be a real turtle. Morrie had sold a little restaurant he'd scrimped by with for years to go into McDonald's with his son, Ron. He thought that now he was going to get out of the woods at last. But his previous place had been a cakewalk compared to this. He couldn't build enough volume to hire a full crew, and he and Ron were working their heads off handling two stations apiece all day long.

Morrie called me on the telephone and raised hell.

"Ray, I am averaging $5,000 a month here," he said. "If I have a real good month it's $7,000. Now that place called Peak's across town is doing $12,000 a month, and they have an inferior location!"

Peak's happened to be a misfit McDonald's, one of the franchises sold by the McDonald brothers before I came into the picture. I suggested to Morrie that he ask the McDonald boys for some guidance. He said O.K., that was a good idea, he'd do it. A few days later he was back on the phone more upset than before.

"This is ridiculous!" he moaned. "I had Maurice and Richard come down from San Bernardino, and they spent most of the day here poking around. They get ready to leave, Ray, and you know what they tell me? They say, 'You are doing everything just right. All you have to do is continue this way and the business will come.' Hellfire, they were no help at all!"

I told Morrie that I would come out again and see if I could figure it out. It was baffling. I studied that place from every angle without coming up with an answer.

Morrie's volume problem continued for about five years. After he got his equipment paid off he had a little breathing space. Then I moved out and opened our California office. We built a lot of new stores and started a local advertising campaign, and that really got things rolling for Morrie. In 1975, his La Tijera store grossed close to a million dollars. He has torn the old store down now and replaced it with a beautiful new building.

I get furious all over again just thinking about that California situation during the first five years we were in business. It was aggravation unlimited. In many ways it was a parallel to the frustrations I faced at home with my wife. The McDonald brothers were simply not on my wavelength at all. I was obsessed with the idea of making McDonald's the biggest and best. They were content with what they had; they didn't want to be bothered with more risks and more demands. But there wasn't much I could do about it, California was simply too far away for me to deal with effectively from Chicago.

At one point I sent Fred Turner out to report on the McDonald brothers' California operations. He came back appalled at the haphazard situation he'd found. The brothers' own store in San Bernardino was virtually the only "pure" McDonald's operation. Others had adulterated the menu with things like pizza, burritos, and enchiladas. In many of them the quality of the hamburgers was inferior, because they were grinding hearts into the meat and the high fat content made it greasy. The McDonald boys just turned their backs on such poor practices. Their operators refused to cooperate with mine in volume purchasing and advertising. We asked them to contribute one percent of their gross toward an advertising campaign that would benefit our stores and all of them as well, but they would have nothing to do with it. All I could do for the time being was to live with it. I am bitter about the experience; not for myself alone, but for fine operators like Morrie Goldfarb and many others who lost five year's growth as a result.

In our business there are two kinds of attitudes toward advertising and public relations. One is the outlook of the begrudger who treats every cent paid for ad programs or publicity campaigns as if they were strictly expenditures. My own viewpoint is that of the promoter; I never hesitate to spend money in this area, because I can see it coming back to me with interest. Of course, it comes back in different forms, and that may be the reason a begrudger can't appreciate it. He has a narrow vision that allows him to see income only in terms of cash in his register. Income for me can appear in other ways; one of the nicest of them is a satisfied smile on the face of a customer. That's worth a lot, because it means that he's coming back, and he'll probably bring a friend. A child who loves our TV commercials and brings her grandparents to a McDonald's gives us two more customers. This is a direct benefit generated by advertising dollars. But the begrudger has a hard time appreciating this—he wants to have his cake and eat it too.

Harry Sonneborn was not a begrudger. He was always willing to spend money to make money. But he liked things neat and theoretically functional; so he was mad as hell at me back in 1957 when I hired a small public relations firm on a retainer of $500 a month. The outlay was an insult in Harry's mind, considering the financial sacrifices he and June were making; the fact that I couldn't tell him exactly what the outfit was going to do for us really threw him into a regular fit. He was justified. But, on the other hand, so was I. That firm, Cooper and Golin, now Golin Communications, is still with us today, and they deserve a lot of the credit for making McDonald's a household word.

There is another characteristic of the begrudger that I have seen appear from time to time. It is a negative outlook that's easy to see in attitudes toward competition. The begrudger regards competition with envy. He wants to learn their secrets and, if possible, undermine them. He'll often go out of his way to give the competition a bad name.

Fortunately, we don't have too many begrudgers in the McDonald's organization. Their style doesn't suit ours, and they don't stay around long. But I have had people with us who seriously proposed that we plant spies in the operations of our competition. Can you imagine? Next thing we'd learn that Ronald McDonald is a double agent! My response to that kind of claptrap has always been that you can learn all you ever need to know about the competition's operation by looking in his garbage cans. I am not above that, let me assure you, and more than once at two o'clock in the morning I have sorted through a competitor's garbage to see how many boxes of meat he'd used the day before, how many packages of buns, and so forth.

My way of fighting the competition is the positive approach. Stress your own strengths, emphasize *quality, service, cleanliness, and value,* and the competition will wear itself out trying to keep up. I've seen it happen many times. Joe Post, whose Springfield, Missouri, McDonald's I mentioned earlier, is a fierce competitor. His success has bred any number of fast-food imitators in the area (it's worth noting in passing how our competition rides on the coattails of our real estate research by locating near our stores, oftentimes right next door). Joe has knocked them out, one after another, not by copying them or by planting spies in their operations, but simply by giving the public the old McDonald's QSC and V.

Competition has from time to time planted spies in our stores. One very prominent franchisor once got hold of a McDonald's operations manual. Word was that he intended to use it to expand his drive-ins to include hamburgers and french fries. My attitude was that competition can try to steal my plans and copy my style. But they can't read my mind; so I'll leave them a mile and a half behind.

A good example of this was the situation we faced with our 200th unit, which was opened August 30, 1960, in Knoxville, Tennessee, by a former marine corps major named Litton Cochran. There was a competing hamburger operation a few doors away, part of a large southern chain, and the day Litton opened his McDonald's his competitor announced a special—five hamburgers for thirty cents. They kept it up for a solid month. Litton wasn't selling any hamburgers, but he was showing a profit because many of the folks who got hamburgers "to go" from the competition were coming to his place for soft drinks and french fries. Litton figured he'd hang in there, the competition couldn't afford to keep it up for long, and his business would pick up as soon as the guy next door backed down. Instead, the competition got tougher. It advertised a new special—10, 10, and 10—hamburger, milk shake, and french fries for ten cents each!

Litton was really staggered by that one. He was president of the Knoxville Marketing and Sales Executives' Club, and some of his associates there were outraged by his competitor's tactics. One of them, a lawyer, told Litton that it was a clear violation of federal trade regulations since this one store in a chain was being used to drive him out of business by cutting prices. The lawyer offered to go to the government and initiate action against the competitor.

It was with this sad story that Litton Cochran appeared in my Chicago office wondering what he should do.

I am sure this big ex-leatherneck may have heard more abrasive language in the course of his marine career, but I think he'll admit that he's never had a more sincere chewing out than I gave him that afternoon.

"Litton, you are getting your ears beat down, and it's not right," I said. "We can agree on that. But I'm going to tell you something I feel very strongly about. The thing that has made this country great is our free enterprise system. If we have to resort to this—bringing in the government—to beat our competition, then we deserve to go broke. If we can't do it by offering a better fifteen-cent hamburger, by being better merchandisers, by providing faster service and a cleaner place, then I would rather be broke tomorrow and out of this business and start all over again in something else."

I could see that my words had made a positive impression. Litton told me later that he could hardly wait to get back to Tennessee and get cracking in his store. I never heard another word from him about problems with competition, which is pretty good considering that he now owns ten McDonald's in Knoxville! He's president of the national alumni association of the University of Tennessee, where he often lectures on marketing, and I'm told he gives a dynamite talk on the virtues of our free enterprise system.

10

Art Trygg was the bosom companion of my late fifties. He had been on the staff of Rolling Green Country Club, where I often ate dinner in those days. I hired him to write a newsletter for our operators, but he soon became my valet and chauffeur as well. We were like boyhood chums. And I needed Art's gruff good humor and sympathetic ear at dinner, because a powerfully distracting new force had swept into my life—I was in love!

Her name was Joni Smith. She lived in St. Paul.

I had gone to the Criterion restaurant up there to meet the owner, Jim Zien, who was interested in becoming a McDonald's franchisee. I found myself having a hard time concentrating on our dinner conversation, however, because of the classy organ music in the background. It set my pianist's spirit twitching and dancing in time to its sprightly rhythms. Finally Jim took me over to introduce me to the organist.

Well!

I was stunned by her blond beauty. Yes, she was married. Since I was married, too, the spark that ignited when our eyes met had to be ignored, but I would never forget it.

I saw her often in the months that followed. Jim Zien's involvement in McDonald's provided an ideal excuse for me to go up there. We progressed from exchanging small talk, to playing duets on piano and organ, to long, earnest conversations in which I poured out my ideas about McDonald's and my plans for the company's future. Joni was a marvelous listener.

Jim Zien finally got his first location going in Minneapolis and, as luck would have it, he hired Joni's husband, Rollie, to be his manager. This led to long telephone consultations between Joni and me. Strictly business, of course, but with an overlay of growing affection. I would be tingling with pleasure from head to toe when I hung up the receiver.

Feeling this way made it impossible for me to go on living with Ethel. I moved out of our home in Arlington Heights to an apartment in the Whitehall. The next step was to propose to Joni that we both get divorced and marry. I knew this would be a difficult question for her to face, because both of us had grown up with a deep respect for religion and propriety, and we both had been brought up to believe in the sanctity of marriage. She couldn't make up her mind. Finally, I decided that one of us would have to make the first move and get a divorce, and it would have to be me.

So I bought my freedom from Ethel. She wound up getting everything I had except my McDonald's stock. She got the house, the car, all the insurance, and $30,000 a year for life. I was happy to pay the alimony. I respected Ethel, she was a lovely person and a wonderful homemaker, and I wanted to be sure she was secure. My immediate problem was raising the attorneys' fees, $25,000 for my lawyer and $40,000 for hers. There was only one way I could get my hands on that kind of money—by selling Prince Castle Sales, the company that had been my birthright as an independent businessman. Harry Sonneborn helped me arrange a transaction in which executives of McDonald's would purchase Prince Castle for $150,000 cash. It was worth far more, but I didn't mind, I had to have the money immediately and my own people would be the beneficiaries of the deal (they subsequently sold the company for about a million dollars).

Now I could marry Joni as soon as she got her divorce. That

thought filled me with glad anticipation. I knew she would need persuasion, but I was certain that she would do it. Nothing so right as our being man and wife could possibly go wrong. So I went up to make my case and watch her face as she considered it. There was nothing in her reaction that dismayed me. In fact, it was more positive than I'd hoped for. Of course, she needed time to think it over. I'd been prepared for that, and I plunged into the press of McDonald's business to relieve the anxiety of waiting.

The most important item in my plans for the company was to end our relationship with the McDonald brothers. This was partly for personal reasons; Mac and Dick were beginning to get on my nerves with their business game playing. For example, I had introduced them to my good friend and paper supplier, Lou Perlman, and they began buying all of their paper products from him, too. They would come to Chicago and visit Lou and ask him to drive them around to see all the McDonald's locations in the area, which he did, but they would not come by corporate headquarters or even call me on the telephone; Lou would fill me in later on where they'd gone and what they'd said.

But the main reason I wanted to be done with the McDonalds was that their refusal to alter any terms of the agreement was a drag on our development. They blamed their attorney for this lack of cooperation, and he and I certainly were at dagger's point all the time; but whatever the reason, I wanted to be free of their hold on me.

I knew from conversations I'd had with Lou Perlman and others that the McDonald boys could be persuaded to sell. Maurice's health had not been the best, and Dick had expressed concern about that and talked about retiring. I wanted to help them retire, but I was afraid of what it might cost me. Harry Sonneborn and I had several long sessions hashing over the pros and cons of it, deciding the best approach to take. Finally, we determined that we would hit them right between the eyes with it. No use shilly-shallying, because their lawyer would only waste a lot of time bickering about it, and we would come out at the same place in the end anyhow.

So I called Dick McDonald and asked him to name their price.

After a day or two he did, and I dropped the phone, my teeth, and everything else. He asked me what the noise was, and I told him that was me jumping out of the 20th floor of the LaSalle-Wacker Building. They were asking $2.7 million!

"We'd like to have a million dollars apiece after taxes, Ray," Dick explained. "That's for all the rights, the name, the San Bernardino store, and everything. You know, we feel we've earned it. We've been in business over thirty years, working seven days a week, week in and week out."

Very touching. But somehow I just couldn't seem to work up any tears of pity.

This was really going to take some financial wheeling and dealing. I asked Harry to take a run at the three insurance companies that had lent us the million and a half dollars. We had to anyhow, because they had a right of first refusal on McDonald's borrowing for a period. But John Gosnell said Paul Revere Life couldn't take any bigger bite than it had, Fred Fideli said State Mutual Life felt the same, and Massachusetts Protective couldn't swing a deal without the other two. So there we were—three strikes and we were out on the street looking for some Santa Claus with a bagful of money.

I was feeling pretty low, so I called Joni and told her about it. I said it would be a lot easier for me if I had her by my side. She said she needed more time. She couldn't make up her mind.

Damn!

Harry found our money man in New York. His name was John Bristol, and he was financial advisor to Princeton University, Howard University, Carnegie Tech, the Ford Foundation and others, a total of twelve educational and charitable institutions. The deal we agreed on, I think, put a new wrinkle in American financial arrangements. Harry was delighted with its intricate design. Here's how it worked:

In return for $2.7 million in cash from Bristol's group (who were called *The Twelve Apostles* in our records) we were to pay them .5 percent of the gross sales of all McDonald's stores in three periods. In the first period we would pay .4 percent immediately and put aside .1 percent until the third period. The method of computing how much of the .4 percent would go to interest was figured on the basis of 6 percent of $2.7 million; whatever remained would go toward retiring the principal. The first period would end when the principal was retired. The second period would be for a length of time equal to the first period, whatever that was. In the second period we would pay a straight .5 percent of our gross. The third period, then, would be the payment of the deferred .1 percent from the first period.

Our original projection sheets anticipated that it would take us until 1991 to pay it all off. But that was on the basis of 1961 volume. We managed to pay off the principal in six years and finished paying off the loan completely in 1972.

It was an extremely successful deal. All concerned were happy. The Twelve Apostles wound up making about $12 million on it, and while that seems like a terrific price to pay, remember that we had been forking over .5 percent to the McDonald brothers all along anyhow. The total cost of the transaction to us—about $14 million—was peanuts compared to what the corporation earned in the years that followed by retaining that .5 percent instead of paying it to Mac and Dick McDonald. On today's systemwide sales of more than $3 billion, that .5 percent would be up there over $15 million a year.

The McDonald brothers retired happily to travel and tend their real estate investments in Palm Springs. Maurice died a few years later and Dick moved back to New Hampshire and married his childhood sweetheart, a pleasant person named Dorothy French, daughter of a Manchester banker. Her first husband had died and Dick and his first wife were divorced, so the reunion was fortunate. I'm told that the marriage has mellowed Dick's New England crustiness to the point where he now recalls our association as "the finest business relationship we ever had."

I was happy too, except for one part of the deal that stuck in my throat like a fishbone. That was the McDonald brother's last minute insistence on retaining their original restaurant in San Bernardino. They were going to have their employees run it for them. What a goddam rotten trick! I needed the income from that store. There wasn't a better location in the entire state. I screamed like hell about it. But no way. They decided they wanted to keep it, and they were willing to pull the plug on the whole arrangement if they didn't get it. Eventually I opened a McDonald's across the street from that store, which they had renamed The Big M, and it ran them out of business. But that episode is why I can't feel charitable or forgiving toward the McDonald brothers. They went back on their promise, made on a handshake, and forced me into grinding it out, grunting and sweating like a galley slave for every inch of progress in California.

California! I was fascinated by the promise I saw out there. The tide of population growth and economic and cultural energy in the country had shifted from the Northeast and was running toward the South and Southwest. I didn't want McDonald's to miss out on that rising crest.

"You know, I've been thinking I ought to go out to California and open an office out there. . . ." I remarked to Art Trygg.

"I knew another guy had ideas like that," my companion said with mock peevishness as he wheeled my Thunderbird through Michigan Avenue traffic. "The doctor told him to soak his head in beer every night, and it cured him."

"Don't you like sunshine, Art?"

"Not if I can get moonshine, Ray."

I have a whole album of mental snapshots from that period. Turning through them brings back a rush of memories. Not nostalgia, but reaffirmation of my faith in McDonald's and the people who helped me build it. I speak of faith in McDonald's as if it were a religion. And, without meaning any offense to the Holy Trinity, the Koran, or the Torah, that's exactly the way I think of it. I've often said that *I believe in God, family, and McDonald's—and in the office, that order is reversed.* If you are running a hundred-yard dash, you aren't thinking about God while you're running. Not if you hope to win. Your mind is on the race. My race is McDonald's.

Mental Snapshot: A thin, solemn young man sits next to my desk. He's clearly nervous. His name is Luigi Salvaneschi and he has not been in this country long. June Martino sponsored his immigration from Italy and got him a job as a crewman in our store in Glen Ellyn, Illinois. I am trying to find out what potential he might have within the corporation. His chief handicap is not his difficulty with the English language—he probably has a bigger vocabulary than I do. His problem is that he is overeducated.

Luigi has a Ph.D. in canon law from the University of Rome and Latin University in the Vatican. He reads ancient Greek for relaxation. When he came to the United States he anticipated getting a university teaching position. His wife, also a Ph.D., was hired by Valparaiso University in Indiana, but Luigi learned to his great astonishment that colleges here are not teaching Latin anymore. They had no need of his specialty, so he stayed with McDonald's and worked his way up from the lowest crew position to manager of the store. His conversation with me is full of explanations of how he has been "culture shocked" by his transition from classic refinement in Rome to a restaurant that is the symbol of a "society on wheels" in which people eat on the move, holding their food in their hands. He thinks the architecture of our red-and-white tile buildings should be redesigned.

Is this guy nuts?

My decision finally was to bring Luigi into the corporation. All that education had given him a complete set of additional things to worry about beyond the normal problems of business, but he seemed to handle them well. Certainly his work record made him a prime candidate to manage one of our new McOpCo stores. One of the things Luigi had done in that Glen Ellyn McDonald's was to teach what may have been the first formal operations lessons in our system. He decided that his crew was not greeting customers properly, so he wrote what he called a "Windowman Lesson" and sat his crew members on shortening cans in the basement to listen to him lecture. He even gave them homework to do and money rewards when they showed improvement.

The idea of holding classes for new operators and managers had occurred to me when I first brought Fred Turner into headquarters. He was enthusiastic about it, too, and it was one of those goals that keep coming up in meetings but are put aside to make room for more pressing things. Fred refused to let the idea get buried, though. He collaborated with Art Bender and one of our field consultants named Nick Karos to compile a training manual for operators. When we were planning to build a company store in Elk Grove Village, a fast-growing development northwest of Chicago, I insisted that it have a full basement instead of the usual partial basement. That was to be the first classroom for courses that eventually would become Hamburger University. There was a motel next to the Elk Grove store so it was convenient for out-of-town operators and managers to stay there while attending classes. They would sit at desk-arm chairs down among the potato sacks and listen to lectures by Nick Karos, Fred Turner, and Tony Felker. At noon the students would apply what they'd learned by doing practical work upstairs in the store. Our first class had eighteen students.* We awarded them a Bachelor of Hamburgerology degree with a minor in french fries.

My God, it was great to be green and growing! To see stories in newspapers across the country recognize our impact on business and praise our operators for their participation in community affairs.

Ours was the kind of story the American public was longing to hear. They'd had enough of doom and gloom and cold war politics. The Soviet Union's blustering announcements of new ballistic missiles and launching of the first satellite, Sputnik, into orbit around the earth had fostered a defensive attitude in our country, and people built bomb shelters in their back yards and read up on what to do in case of nuclear attack. In the fall of 1959 Soviet Premier Nikita Khrushchev told the United Nations Gen-General Assembly, and the world, banging his shoe on his desk for emphasis, that his nation's system would bury capitalism.

---

* Ten are still with us as McDonald's licensees: Mel Foerster, Louis Groen, Don Hazeltine, Ralph Lanphar, Jack Lubeznik, Dick Picchietti, Frank Patton, Chuck Posey, Dick Shepard, and Reub Taylor. Others in the class were: Barney Agate, Tony Fellier, Ted Hoffman, Bob Kinsley, Earl McGill, Bill Stachols, John Syyperski, and Al Wooliford.

Shortly after that Irv Kupcinet wrote in his *Chicago Sun-Times* column:

> Nine sailors, soon to be discharged from Great Lakes, called on Ray Kroc, head of McDonald's Drive-ins, at his LaSalle Street offices the other day. They related that they had entered the service together, were leaving together, and wanted to go into business together. Kroc obliged them. The nine sailors will be partners in a McDonald's franchise in Portland, Ore. This is what Ray Kroc means by fulfillment of the American capitalist dream. See, Khrushchev?

I've held a lot of press conferences and given a lot of interviews during the growth of McDonald's throughout the country, but one of the most memorable was set up by Al Golin with the late Associated Press columnist Hal Boyle. I knew Boyle only by reputation as a Pulitzer-Prize-winning war correspondent whose column seemed to show up in papers in just about every city I visited. I didn't know that he was one of New York's more disorganized writers, and I was blissfully unaware of Al Golin's agonies over the fact that Boyle had forgotten about our appointment and wanted to "do it some other time." Al did tell me there'd been a problem, and we would have to do the interview in Boyle's office instead of over lunch.

That was okay by me, but I wasn't prepared for this big room with clattering typewriters and teletype printers. You could hardly hear yourself think. And there was Boyle, looking like a fun-loving Irish bartender behind a desk covered with what one of his colleagues had described as "a sacred pile of debris, which is said to conceal the first of the Dead Sea Scrolls and the last of Judge Crater."* Boyle shoved a pile of papers from a chair and asked me to sit down. I chose the edge of a desk. My public relations man looked a bit dismayed, but I didn't mind. I'd come to tell the story of McDonald's and I did, raising my voice to carry over the background noise. One by one the other reporters and

---

* A New York judge who mysteriously disappeared in 1930.

editors left what they were doing and gathered around Boyle's desk. By the time I finished talking the room was quiet. There was a crowd listening, and several of them wanted to know how they could get out of the newspaper business and become McDonald's operators. Boyle was impressed, too. His column started this way:

> America has gone mad over pizza pies, but in less than five years Ray Kroc has built up a 25-million-dollar business in an older U.S. food favorite—the hamburger. "I put the hamburger on the assembly line," said Kroc, 56, president of a chain that now sells 100 million 15-cent hamburgers a year.

It went on to tell how I'd developed the system, and it closed with these observations:

> Kroc says his spectacularly successful hamburger emporiums average a net of $40,000 on an annual gross of $200,000. The average customer's check is 66 cents. "Not one franchise has failed ... we don't see how one could," he said crisply. "In any case, we wouldn't let it. We'd come in and take over."

What none of these stories mentioned, and I wasn't about to tell anyone, was that even though our stores were booming, and even though our "development accounting" allowed us to show a profit, we had no cash flow. We were in the trough between our heavy outlays for land and buildings and the income in rents from those properties. Of our first 160 stores, only 60 were units for which we had developed the restaurants and were receiving income above the service fee. The rest were units in which the operators themselves owned the restaurants, and they paid us only the 1.9 percent service fee. This put us in a rather paradoxical situation. Our gross sales figures continued to climb, and many individual units were prospering. One store in Minneapolis chalked up a then incredible one-month sale of $37,262. At the same time, we were barely able to meet our payrolls in corporate headquarters. Harry Sonneborn issued an order that no bill for more than a thousand dollars would be paid in full. Anything over a thousand would be paid in monthly installments.

That was the situation when Dick Boylan decided to hire a young accountant named Gerry Newman. Dick had developed into Harry Sonneborn's understudy—Harry didn't spend a nickel or even sneeze, it seemed, without telling Boylan what he was doing and why. He wanted to make sure his deals would be carried out if he should happen to get run over by a truck. We needed someone with experience in construction accounting who could analyze our costs. Newman had handled books on brick-and-mortar and plumbing businesses, so Boylan brought him aboard. Gerry had wanted to handle us as one of several accounts, but he soon found that our work load left little time for other clients. That would have been all right if we'd been able to compensate him for it. But we couldn't. All we had to offer was more work. We had forty-five people in our office then, and their cost was more than our revenue. The week finally came that we were overdrawn at our bank and couldn't meet our payroll. Gerry's solution was to switch the pay period from weekly to bimonthly. He posted a notice on the bulletin board that anyone who was strapped by not getting their check that Friday could borrow up to $15 from petty cash.

Mental Snapshot: I am sitting in Dick Boylan's office with Dick and Harry and this new kid, Gerry Newman. I don't know much about him, but I'm told he's bright as hell. We are having a late-evening conference about accounting. Art Trygg arrives from the Singapore with a load of barbecued ribs and other goodies, and this gets us off the subject of bookkeeping, for which I am grateful, because what I really want to talk about is the tremendous sales volumes our units around the country are reporting.

"Listen," I say, "one of these days we are going to hit grosses of $100,000 a month! We're gonna be a billion-dollar company!"

Newman is frozen by that statement, stopped in mid-bite. He looks at me with this funny, pop-eyed expression.

Years later I learned that Gerry had gone home and told his wife, Bobbi, that he had met me that night, and I had to be either a nut or a dreamer or both. Here he was worried about whether we'd still be in business the next week, and I was carrying on about the billions of dollars in our future. A year or so after that incident, Gerry was offered a job by another drive-in chain at twice the salary he was getting from us. He turned it down. When the disbelieving head hunter asked why, he said, "Because you don't have a Ray Kroc."

But it took more than belief in me for Gerry to stay with us. It also took daring and a personal vision. Gerry has a mind that's much like mine in certain respects. He has a strong memory that gives him total recall of situations. Unlike me, however, he's also a squirrel with reports and odd pieces of paper. As a result, he is able to answer virtually any question one could ask about McDonald's. He even remembers some things that I forget, and that's rare.

Cynics say everything has its price. I say poppycock! There are things money can't buy and hard work can't win. One of them is happiness. There's a slippery notion for you! Would I have been happy if I'd never met Joni Smith? I don't know. Certainly I was fulfilled in my work. It was my life. Yet, having met her, I realized there was something missing. So I went after it. I would have given anything. I would even have dropped McDonald's to win her. But money had no value in this quest. All I could do was wait and hope that she would come to me.

Finally, after what seemed like months, Joni called to tell me she'd made up her mind. Rather, her daughter and her mother had helped her make up her mind. They were both strongly opposed to her getting a divorce, and she couldn't bring herself to break with them. So her answer was no. . . . A giant fissure cracked the concrete of LaSalle Street, and our office building crumbled into it as thunder rolled and lightning cracked over the smoking ruins! I was the only one who felt it, of course, but that made the agony a hundred times worse. I sat there alone for hours, ignoring the ringing of the telephone, watching the daylight wane and streetlights come on. Then I heard Art Trygg calling to me from the outer office. He stood in the door looking at me quizzically.

"Get your bags packed, Art," I told him. "We're going to California!"

11

I made Harry Sonneborn president and chief executive officer of McDonald's in 1959, when he negotiated the $1.5 million loan with the three insurance companies. I continued as chairman, and we worked substantially as equals. Harry's sphere was financial and administrative matters. Mine was the retail end—operations, dealing with suppliers, and so forth. Our interests and control overlapped when it came to seeking out sites and developing them. The two of us were the only officers with authority to close a transaction for a new location.

My view was that this relationship and relatively smooth-running division of responsibilities would continue when I moved to California. I'm not sure exactly what Harry thought, but I believe his opinion was that I had removed myself from the command center to go off on what, at heart, he considered a fool's errand. At any rate, as time passed he became increasingly bullheaded and willful, and we began clashing on all kinds of trivial as well as important issues. The only thing that kept us together, finally, was the diplomacy of June Martino. When Harry would countermand one of my directives, leaving some young executive between a rock and a hard place, June would work it out with us individually. She became known in office gossip as "The Vice-President of Equilibrium." Needless to say, it was not long before this began affecting morale in the organization, especially in Chicago. It also caused the gradual creation of an unwritten organizational chart in which executives were identified as Kroc people or Sonneborn people. Harry brought in a hard-driving real estate operative named Pete Crow, who with others formed the nucleus of the Sonneborn faction.

I could see this situation forming like a glacier beginning to build in the Chicago office, but there wasn't a damned thing I could do about it. I had my hands full with the boar's nest of problems I found in California. In the end, my California project was worth the effort. The position of the area for McDonald's changed between 1961 and 1967 from an insignificant cluster of stores to a dynamic market, equal in development and volume to the rest of the country. But it took me fully three years to get the mess unraveled and headed in the right direction. First off, because Los Angeles had been the cradle of drive-in restaurants, and they had grown so wildly throughout the region, the industry had accumulated more corrupt habits than a flophouse janitor. Suppliers had formed a series of cartels and managed to push prices out of sight. For example, the same buns we were paying twenty cents for in Chicago were going for forty cents in L.A. Meat was the same way. But meat was even worse, because of the dramatic fluctuations in supply. When beef grew scarce, fast-food operators began performing the ancient ritual known as turning pockets inside out. To make matters more difficult, California distributors took it for granted that a franchisor walked around with his hand out for kickbacks in exchange for granting exclusive contracts. The distributor always made out, because he would get back the amount of the payoff and maybe even a little extra in increased prices to the franchisee.

Convincing these people that we were an honest operation, that we protected our operators, and that we would take no kickbacks, was a big order. They could not be persuaded that if they would supply McDonald's restaurants with items the way we wanted them at prices that would allow us to sell hamburgers for fifteen cents, our growth would put them on Easy Street. McDonald's had no identity as a system out there, and that sharpened the other barb of our problem—low volume.

> *Mental Snapshot:* Nick Karos, field consultant, one of the group of executives I'd brought with me from Chicago to help develop California, is standing on the corner in front of an invitingly clean McDonald's where we are doing zero business. Nick has one foot up on a fireplug, and he is watching the flow of people in bizarre-looking cars and the pedestrians walking brightly ribboned dogs, typical Angelinos in their habitat. He says to me, "Ray, the reason we can't pull people in here is because these golden arches blend right into the landscape. People don't even see them. We have to do something different to get their attention."
>
> "Okay, Nick," I reply. "Lemme know when you find the solution."

Nick did come up with a proposal, but it wasn't the next day, or even the next year. As one of Fred Turner's favorite sayings has it, we were up to our asses in alligators, and in that situation it is difficult to remember that your objective is to drain the swamp. First we had to get our supply problem solved. Nick Karos was a big help there. He was a griddle-savvy guy who had grown up in a Wimpy's restaurant that his father owned in Joliet, Illinois. He'd come to us from operating a Henry's hamburger stand in Chicago, and he did a lot of field work for us in the St. Louis area, where he'd dealt with the Freund bakery people. It happened that Harold Freund had retired to California. So Nick looked him up and introduced him to me. As I mentioned earlier, I had a hell of a time persuading Harold to go back into business and build a bakery to serve McDonald's operators. But he did, at last, and our financial prospects brightened immediately.

At the same time, I was looking for a meat purveyor. My choice was a fellow I had known from my years of traveling before I started McDonald's System. His name was Bill Moore, and he had a company called Golden State Foods. Bill had bought out his partner in the firm the year before I moved to California, and he'd lost money for thirteen straight months. His plant and equipment were outdated, and he needed capital. His approach was to try and get me to buy Golden State Foods. I turned that off quickly, explaining that I didn't want McDonald's in the supply business.

"Well, then," he said, "I need about a million dollars to keep from going under. You've done a fair amount of borrowing. What do you think I should do?"

"Listen, Bill," I said, "you hang on here. We have fifteen stores now, and pretty soon we'll have a hundred. You'll be able to get back on your feet and expand right along with us."

He agreed, and that's exactly what happened. In fact, Bill Moore is a good example of what McDonald's has done for the suppliers who came with us and helped us grow. In 1965 he and a partner bought a McDonald's franchise in San Diego, a market I was dubious about because it was the home turf of the Jack-in-the-Box chain, which had about thirty locations there. Burger Chef had broken its spatula trying to compete with them. Bill and his partner had a slow start, but they made it. In just over two years they developed four more stores and were really cooking with gas when the partner dropped dead of a heart attack. We bought back all five units for stock. A couple of years later Bill sold the stock for enough money to build a large manufacturing and warehouse complex in City of Industry, California. His meat plant there now processes 300 million hamburger patties a year for McDonald's restaurants, and in addition, he makes syrup for soft drinks and manufactures milk-shake mix. He also has gone into distribution for McDonald's units. He perfected the one-stop service idea, in which a truck pulls up to one of our stores and fills all its needs, like an old-fashioned grocery store delivery truck, with a single call. This results in great savings for both parties. Bill has another plant and warehouse in Atlanta and distribution centers in San Jose, California, and in North Carolina and Hawaii.

I could tell the same sort of story about most of the suppliers who started with us in the early days and grew right along with us. Lou Perlman, our paper supplier, also went back a long way with me. He and I used to call on the same customers when I was selling Multimixers and he was peddling paper products. We attended the same conventions, and we became friends. So it was only natural that I went to him when I was starting McDonald's and asked him to come up with a program of paper products imprinted with the McDonald's logo.

Lou and I shook hands on an arrangement that grew and multiplied for both of us. He began supplying McDonald's operators with a complete line of paper goods, and his Perlman Paper Company became a subsidiary of Martin-Brower Corporation. He was chairman of the board of Martin-Brower when he retired.

Harry Smargon, our shortening supplier, is another case in point. I was introduced to his product by accident. A fellow named Dick Keating was trying to sell me the kind of french fryer he made, and I was impressed—we still use Keating fryers to this day—but I was equally impressed with the quality of shortening used in the demonstration. So I found out about Harry Smargon and Interstate Foods, the young company he'd started three years earlier, and I telephoned him and asked for a thirty-pound sample. It wasn't long before McDonald's stores were ordering thousands of pounds of shortening from Interstate Foods. Naturally, Harry was delighted. He had been in the wholesale coffee business before he started Interstate, and experience there had taught him that customers often gave him an account because they wanted something extra, a sign, a clock, a coffee urn, or some such thing. So he telephoned one day and said he'd like to meet the man who was giving him so much business. Fine, come on down, I said.

I could tell Harry was surprised at the tiny size of our office on LaSalle Street. I introduced him to June Martino, and we exchanged pleasantries for a time. Finally he said, "Ray, I've been getting a lot of business from you, and I'd like to show you my appreciation. I'd like to give you something for your stores—a sign or a clock—what would you like?"

"Listen, Harry, you don't know me, so I am going to forgive you for that," I said. "But let's get this straight, once and for all. I want nothing from you but a good product. Don't wine me, don't dine me, don't buy me any Christmas presents. If there are any cost breaks, pass them on to the operators of McDonald's stores."

Harry Smargon has prospered with McDonald's, and I never heard him so much as hint at a kickback again.

Gene Veto, our insurance man, was introduced to me by June Martino. We had sixteen restaurants franchised at the time, and there were about fifty or sixty insurance policies covering them. I knew we had a mess on our hands, but I didn't know what to do about it. Gene took our portfolio home and spent about a week analyzing it. He returned with a report that pointed out duplications, areas where we needed more protection, and some overcharges. I thought it was a terrific report, and I pointed out that he had forgotten to bill us for it.

He said, "I'm not going to send you a bill. I don't think you can afford it. But you've got a great concept here, and I think we'll be able to do some business in the future. I'll be in touch."

As a matter of fact, Gene wound up reorganizing the insurance coverage for our franchised stores and later developed a plan whereby we could pool a number of our restaurants, regardless of location, and take advantage of discounts. His Keeler Insurance company grew right along with McDonald's. In 1974 when Keeler became a division of the Frank B. Hall Company, Gene was named chairman of the board.

There are few things more gratifying to me than to see a meat plant like the one operated by Arthur and Lenny Kolschowsky in Chicago. It was built so they could offer McDonald's operators in the Midwest millions of pounds of frozen patties. I can remember buying my first pound of ground beef for my Des Plaines store from the boys' father, Otto Kolschowsky, in his neighborhood butcher shop!

As we solved our supply problems in California and built more stores, business gradually picked up. But it remained far lower than it should have been. In midsummer of 1963, Nick Karos came to me with a proposal he had drafted for a television advertising campaign. The projected cost was $180,000 and he wanted to pay for it by raising the price of hamburgers in our company-owned stores a penny, from fifteen to sixteen cents.

"Nick, this is a terrific plan," I said. "But we're not gonna raise the price. What I want you to do is go back to Chicago and present this to Harry Sonneborn. Make him come up with the money."

I knew he'd be able to do it, because the logic of his one page memo was irrefutable. It demonstrated precisely how an ad campaign would repay its cost many times over, while failing to spend the money would cost us much more in the long run. Nick was successful, although Harry went along very reluctantly. The advertising campaign we put together was a smash hit. It turned Californians into our parking lots as though blindfolds had been removed from their eyes, and suddenly they could see the golden arches. That was a big lesson for me in the effectiveness of television.

As we began to turn the corner in California, the corporation as a whole was starting to reap the benefits of our earlier planning and investments. By 1963 we had gotten over the hump of front-end outlay for leased and purchased properties, and they were beginning to pay us some handsome returns.

Also by this time our program of building and operating company stores was in its third year and had shifted into high gear. It too was contributing significantly to our mounting profits.

Hamburger University had meshed fully into our system by 1963 and was sending a steady procession of qualified operators and managers into the field, where they spread the gospel of *Quality, Service, Cleanliness, and Value.* Classes had grown to an average of twenty-five or thirty students, and we were holding eight to ten two-week sessions a year. Hamburger U was also helping to test and implement training procedures on new equipment that was being developed by our Research and Development Laboratory in Addison, Illinois.

Louis Martino, June's engineer husband, had started the R&D lab in 1961. He'd had extensive in-store experience as an operator in Glen Ellyn, Illinois, and he saw the need for more sophisticated mechanical equipment and electronic aids to speed up our food assembly line and make our products more uniform. His first project was the development of a computer to time the blanching of french fries. We had a recipe for blanching that called for pulling the potatoes out of the oil when they got a certain color and grease bubbles formed a certain way. It was amazing that we got them as uniform as we did, because each kid working the fry vats would have his own interpretation of the proper color and so forth. Louis's computer took all the guesswork out of it, modifying the frying time to suit the balance of water to solids in a given batch of potatoes. He also engineered a dispenser that allowed us to squirt exactly the right amount of catsup and mustard onto our premeasured hamburger patties. Our insistence that beef used to make our patties be no more than nineteen percent fat had been difficult to enforce. We had to take relatively large samples to some laboratory and have it tested. This changed with the development of the Fatilyzer, a simple but precise testing device that an operator could use to analyze meat right in his store. If it was more than nineteen percent fat, he would reject an entire shipment. After this happened to a supplier a few times, he would get the message and improve his own quality controls.

All of this progress was very rewarding.

I should have been elated.

We had a fine, hard-working staff in California—Bob Whitney handled real estate; Gene Bolton, legal; Bob Papp, construction; and Nick Karos, operations. The office was enlivened by the pranks of my fun-loving secretary, Mary Torigian. It was a hell of a contrast to the austere mood of the Chicago office. One morning, for example, I came to work to find Colonel Sanders sitting outside my door typing away. It was Mary wearing a Kentucky Fried Chicken halloween mask. I didn't say a word. I walked right by her and bopped her on the head with my rolled up newspaper as I passed.

I should have been happy, but the undeniable fact was that I was miserable. I had forced Joni out of my mind, but I could not get her out of my heart. She and her husband had long since moved to Rapid City, South Dakota, to open McDonald's stores of their own, and I knew they were doing very well from the daily financial reports I received on all our operations.

I wondered if she missed me as much as I missed her. After Art Trygg went back to Chicago, I was really lonely. He had a girlfriend there, a spinster who worked in our real estate department, so I couldn't blame him for not wanting to stay in California.

I moved out of my apartment into a home in Woodland Hills. I busied myself in buying furniture and fixing the place up with all kinds of conveniences for gracious living. I have never been a cliff dweller, I told myself. But down deep, I think I did it with the subconscious hope that Joni would change her mind, and we would live there together.

One thing I liked about that house was that it perched on a hill looking down on a McDonald's store on the main thoroughfare. I could pick up a pair of binoculars and watch business in that store from my living room window. It drove the manager crazy when I told him about it. But he sure had one hell of a hard-working crew!

Some people are bachelors by nature. I am not. I guess I need to be married to feel complete. That's why I fell so hard for Jane.

Her name was Jane Dobbins Green. She was John Wayne's secretary. A mutual friend introduced us, and I was charmed by Jane's sweet disposition. She was lovely, a sort of diminutive Doris Day, and she was completely opposite to Joni in manner. Joni is a strong person who knows her own mind. Jane was compliant: If the sky was clear and I said it looked like rain, Jane would agree.

We had dinner together the night after we met, and the next night, and the night after that. In fact, we had dinner together five nights in a row. I was enchanted. Within two weeks we were married.

Of course, Joni, found out about it eventually. One day I got a telephone call from her and we had a brief, businesslike conversation that she ended by asking, "Ray, are you happy?"

I was shaken and astonished. It took me a moment to catch my voice. Then I blurted, "Yes!" and slammed down the receiver.

12

Jane and I sold our place in Woodland Hills and moved to a big house in Beverly Hills. I wasn't around there much though, because when you're green and growing at the rate McDonald's was in 1963, there's little time for personal interests. We topped all previous construction records in 1963 by building 110 stores scattered all over the country, and we did even better the following year when we had a net income of $2.1 million on sales of $129.6 million. I became a regular commuter between Los Angeles and corporate headquarters, spending two weeks at a time in L.A. and the next week in Chicago.

I had to take a more active role at headquarters, because the operations were expanding so rapidly and because Harry had withdrawn from day-to-day business in the office to spend all his time studying how we could take the company public.

Harry and Dick Boylan had talked to some large corporations, including Consolidated Foods, Holiday Inns, and United Fruit about the possibility of merger. There was a fad for mergers at that time, and there were certain advantages to be gained from

135

merging with an already public company, as opposed to going public by ourselves. These negotiations never got very far, because the only condition under which Harry or I would agree to merge was if McDonald's would be the surviving company.

The reason for going public, in addition to raising capital for the company was to give us some funds ourselves. We had put this tremendous money-generating machine in motion, and it was running at a fantastic rate. But we hadn't been taking anything out, we were plowing it all back, so as not to slow down the company's expansion.

So Harry spent his days closeted in meetings with bankers, brokers, and lawyers. I was busy trying to decentralize our management structure. We had 637 stores now, and it was unwieldy to supervise them all from Chicago. It has always been my belief that authority should be placed at the lowest possible level. I wanted the man closest to the stores to be able to make decisions without seeking directives from headquarters.

Harry didn't quite see things my way in these matters. He wanted tighter corporate controls, a more authoritarian posture. I maintained that authority should go with a job. Some wrong decisions may be made as a result, but that's the only way you can encourage strong people to grow in an organization. Sit on them and they will be stifled. The best ones will go elsewhere. I knew that very well from my past experience with John Clark at Lily Tulip Cup. I believe that *less is more* in the case of corporate management; for its size, McDonald's today is the most unstructured corporation I know, and I don't think you could find a happier, more secure, harder working group of executives anywhere.

My solution to our administrative problem was simply to divide the country into regions. There were to be five of them, but we decided to establish the West Coast Region of fourteen states first, because it was growing faster and was the most difficult to administer from Chicago. I chose Steve Barnes to be our first regional manager.

Steve had joined McDonald's in 1961 from Lou Perlman's company, where he'd sold us paper products. He had come to my attention in 1962 for the pioneering work he was doing in developing frozen french fries in collaboration with a fellow named Ken Strong, who now heads our food research lab in California.

The idea of using frozen french fries appealed to me greatly. It could assure us a continuous supply of the best potatoes, Idaho Russett Burbanks, because we could conceivably purchase and process an entire crop without fear of spoilage. Shipping costs would be a lot lower, and the square boxes of frozen potatoes would be much easier to handle and store than 100-pound bags. It also would eliminate two messy and time consuming tasks in our stores—peeling the potatoes and blanching them.

There were diehards in our organization who thought that the only good french fry was one made from a fresh potato. For them there was something mysterious, almost sacred, in the rites of peeling, washing the starch out, and blanching. I was to blame for this attitude, I suppose, because I had put so much emphasis on it, and I insisted that our classes at Hamburger U. make it a ritual.

But for an operator to insist on peeling his own potatoes in the store instead of using a frozen product was on the same order as insisting on slaughtering his own steers and grinding the hamburger. Not quite as messy, of course, but potato peelings gave us plenty of problems nevertheless. At least one store had failed and some others were in serious difficulty because of potato peelings. These were outlying units in areas where septic tank fields functioned less than perfectly due to the character of the local soil. Our potatoes were peeled by carborundum wheels and the fine waste was washed into the septic system. Whew! what an odor! No stable in the world could stink worse than a rich vein of fermenting potato peelings. And customers tend to avoid a restaurant that's going aswamp in its own sludge.

Of course, the quality of our french fries was a large part of McDonald's success, and I certainly didn't want to jeopardize our business with a frozen potato that was not up to our standard. So we made certain that the frozen product was thoroughly tested and that it met every condition of quality before we made it part of the system.

There was another product being tested at this time that would prove to have a tremendous effect on our business. This was the

Filet-O-Fish sandwich. It had been born of desperation in the mind of Louis Groen in Cincinnati. He had that city as an exclusive territory as a result of some horse trading he'd done with Harry and me back in the days when we were using everything but butterfly nets to catch franchisees. Lou's major competition was the Big Boy chain. They dominated the market. He managed to hold his own against them, however, on every day but Friday. Cincinnati has a large Catholic population and the Big Boys had a fish sandwich. So if you add those two together on a day the church had ordained should be meatless, you have to subtract most of the business from McDonald's.

My reaction when Lou first broached the fish idea to me was, "Hell no! I don't care if the Pope himself comes to Cincinnati. He can eat hamburgers like everybody else. We are not going to stink up our restaurants with any of your damned old fish!"

But Lou went to work on Fred Turner and Nick Karos. He convinced them that he was either going to have to sell fish or sell the store. So they went through a lot of research, and finally made a presentation that convinced me.

Al Bernardin, who was our food technologist at the time, worked with Lou on the type of fish to be used, halibut or cod, and they finally decided to go with the cod. I didn't care for that; it brought back too many childhood memories of cod liver oil, so we investigated and found out it was perfectly legal to merchandise it as North Atlantic whitefish, which I liked better. There were all kinds of fishhooks in developing this sandwich: how long to cook it, what type of breading to use, how thick it should be, what kind of tartar sauce to use, and so forth. One day I was down in our test kitchen and Al told me about a young crew member in Lou Groen's store who had eaten a fish sandwich with a slice of cheese on it.

"Of course!" I exclaimed. "That's exactly what this sandwich needs, a slice of cheese. No, make it half a slice." So we tried it, and it was delicious. And that is how the slice of cheese got into the McDonald's Filet-O-Fish.

We started selling it only on Fridays in limited areas, but we got so many requests for it that in 1965 we made it available in all our stores every day, advertising it as the "fish that catches people." I told Fred Turner and Dick Boylan, both of whom happen to be Catholic, "You fellows just watch. Now that we've invested in all this equipment to handle fish, the Pope will change the rules." A few years later, damned if he didn't. But it only made those big fish sales figures that much sweeter to read.

I have a pretty well developed set of taste buds, and I can usually predict, as with the cheese on fish, the kind of food combinations the public will like. But once in a while I miss the strike zone. That's what happened with the Hulaburger, which I was taking bets would do better than Filet-O-Fish. The Hulaburger was two slices of cheese with a slice of grilled pineapple on a toasted bun. Delicious! I still have one for lunch at home from time to time. But it was a giant flop when we tried it in our stores. One customer said, "I like the hula, but where's the burger?" Well, you can't win 'em all.

McDonald's had a very good year in 1964, but a pall was cast on it for me by Art Trygg's death from cancer. He had been a wonderful friend, always ready to share a joke or help with a problem. When I went to the office one Sunday and accidentally caught my hand in my car door, lopping off the end of one finger, Art was the one I called to take me to the hospital.

Mental Snapshot: Art Trygg and I are sitting alone at my favorite table in the dining room at Rolling Green Country Club. I have just asked him to come to work for me, and he gets this peculiar, stricken look on his face. "There's something you don't know about me, Mr. Kroc," he says, and he proceeds to explain that he is an ex-convict. It seems he drove a beer truck for the old Touhy gang in Chicago during Prohibition and was busted twice. The second time got him a stretch in Stateville Penitentiary. I slap my knee and exclaim, "What the hell, that doesn't matter! You paid for your mistake, so forget about it." He beams happily and says, "Okay, when do I start?"

I appreciated Art's honesty. I like people who level with me and speak their minds. I always say exactly what I think; it's a trait that's gotten me in trouble plenty of times, but I never have problems getting to sleep at night with a guilty conscience. That's why I could never be a politician. People have told me from time to time that I should run for President. They think I could run the country with the same integrity and sound business sense that I gave to McDonald's. I know it wouldn't work. Not that I think a politician has to be dishonest—but he has to compromise some things he believes in strongly for the sake of political expediency. I could not do that.

Art's death troubled me in another way, too. I could not help but recall those many bachelor dinners when I would tell him about Joni like some lovesick schoolboy. I was content with Jane. She was a fine lady, but it was Joni I loved and knew I always would.

Fortunately, there was little time to dwell on death and things that might have been. Business was bursting out the tops of our charts. We were entering the year of our tenth anniversary, and it looked like we were just getting started.

In one critical way that was true. We were about to go public, and that boiled down to what had to be the most traumatic ten days our company had ever experienced. Harry and Dick had settled on Paine, Webber, Jackson & Curtis to be the underwriters of the issue, and there had been a lot of bickering back and forth over details of the deal for months. For one thing, the underwriters insisted that we must have one of the "big eight" accounting firms do our books. We had dealt with Al Doty's company in Chicago for ten years. Both Harry and I wanted to continue with him, but they were adamant. Finally, Harry gave in and elected to go with the firm of Arthur Young & Company. Al Doty continued to do my personal accounting and still does, and June Martino's and Harry Sonneborn's, too. Our attorneys on the public offering were Dey Watts and Pete Coladarci from Chapman & Cutler. They worked very closely with Harry, of course, and that relationship was to make me uncomfortable in later dealings with them.

Our big problem was that our "Development Accounting" method was not certifiable, in the opinion of our accountants. So our books had to be completely redone to show what our earnings would have been without that accounting. We had less than two weeks to go back through the transactions of all previous years and bring the financial statements up to date. Gerry Newman and his staff worked virtually around the clock for ten days straight. The report was completed four hours before the deadline and was flown to Washington, D.C. in our company plane. It just made it under the wire.

Our biggest argument with the underwriters was on what the initial selling price should be. We had split the stock a thousand to one by that time, and the underwriters thought we should go out at seventeen times earnings. I wouldn't stand for that. I knew we were worth more, and I stood to lose more than anyone else if we went out too low. Harry agreed. He fought for twenty times earnings, and he made several trips between New York and Chicago trying to get them to see it our way. It was a stalemate. We had come down to the final deadline when I walked into Harry's office and told everyone involved that there was no way we would go for less than twenty. That was a pretty heavy moment. But I meant it; even if we had to flush away all the hours and weeks of effort that had got us to this point, I was determined not to sell McDonald's short. No way!

So we went on the market at $22.50 a share, and it shot up to $30 before trading ended that first day. The issue was over-subscribed—a tremendous success. Before the first month ended, it had climbed to $50 a share, and Harry, June, and I were wealthier than we'd ever dreamed possible.

Harry was as happy with the outcome as I was, but he wasn't satisfied with having our stock listed over-the-counter. He wanted to see McDonald's up there with the bluest chips on the big board. The New York Stock Exchange had some pretty tough requirements. You had to have so many shareholders in a certain geographic distribution, and you had to have a certain number of round-lot (100 shares or more) shareholders. I really didn't care that much about it. I went along with Harry on the basis that the New York was the class listing, where McDonald's ought to be. But it struck me that some of these folks he was dealing with about it were codfish aristocrats who weren't too sure they wanted to deal with a company that sold fifteen-cent hamburgers. If so, to hell with them! At any rate, we were accepted, and to celebrate, Harry and his new wife, Aloyis, and June Martino and Al Golin all ate hamburgers on the floor of the New York Stock Exchange. Boy! That got terrific coverage in the newspapers. Not only because of the hamburgers, but Aloyis and June were among the first women ever allowed on the floor of the exchange.

This was in July 1966, a year in which we broke through the top of our charts again with $200 million in sales, and the scoreboards on the golden arches in front of all our stores flipped to "OVER 2 BILLION SOLD." Cooper and Golin sent out a blitz of press releases interpreting the magnitude of this event for a space-conscious public. "If laid end-to-end," they enthused, "Two billion hamburgers would circle the earth 5.4 times!" Great fun. Even Harry Sonneborn got caught up in the spirit of promoting McDonald's, and he pulled off a stunt that made me proud of him. He wanted to have us represented in the big Macy's Thanksgiving Day parade in New York, and he approved the concept of a McDonald's All-American High School Band, made up of the two best musicians from each state and the District of Columbia. Then he hired the world's biggest drum and had it shipped by flatcar from a university in Texas. While it was enroute, and the subject of a lot of publicity generated by the parade's promoters, Harry and Al Golin were having a new drumskin made with *McDonald's All-American Band* imprinted on it. It was a huge success. So was the introduction of our clown, Ronald McDonald, who made his national television debut in the parade. Harry followed that coup with another—sponsoring the first Superbowl telecast.

Pretty heady stuff. But there was real substance under all the hoopla. We had our first stock split in April 1966, and I told our first annual stockholders meeting as a public company the following month that we had created a new American institution. I also stressed that it was our strict adherence to moral principles in business that made us so strong.

The steady expansion of our business had another effect, one we hadn't foreseen. We simply outgrew our red-and-white tile buildings. There also appeared to be a movement among our customers away from the idea of eating in their cars. So we decided to experiment with larger buildings and inside seating.

As Jim Schindler declared in a presentation he made on the subject, "It's obvious that our present equipment will not support the kind of volume we are going to do."

Our first store with inside seating opened in Huntsville, Alabama, in July 1966. It was pretty primitive compared to the kind of seating we have now—a narrow counter with stools and a couple or three small tables—but it was a big step forward.

I had put Luigi Salvaneschi in charge of real estate in California when Bob Whitney left us, a choice that was greeted with a lot of headshaking and raised eyebrows back in Chicago. But they didn't know Luigi like I did. He had taken over the first McOpCo store I built when I moved to California in 1961, the Manhattan Beach unit, and he ran it like a veteran. Luigi was always after me to improve the architecture of our buildings.

"Mr. Kroc, California is setting the trend for the rest of the country in community planning," he'd say. "How can we go into these towns and propose to put up these slant-roof buildings, which are absolute eyesores?"

I'd usually wind up getting mad and throwing him out of my office when he started carrying on about aesthetics and Michelangelo and blah, blah, blah. Yet, down deep, I knew he was right. The time was coming that we were going to have to make a major change in the appearance of our buildings. But I was biding my time, letting the need ripen, because I knew that this was going to mean a big battle between Harry Sonneborn and me. I could smell it coming, and I wanted to be ready for it on every front when it happened.

13

There is a cross you must bear if you intend to be head of a big corporation: you lose a lot of your friends on the way up.

It's lonely on top.

I never felt this so keenly as when Harry Sonneborn and I had our final confrontation, and he resigned.

Recalling the various elements of this situation is like thinking about a set of Chinese boxes, each one nesting inside another. When the last one is removed, you are left with an empty box, a sense of loss.

Harry was in poor health. He had a chronic bad back. He also had severe diabetes. Once he was laid up with his back for a whole week in some remote little town in western Canada. He couldn't be flown out; he had to be put on a train. No taxis or rental cars in the town, so he bought a Cadillac, paid cash for it, and had his wife drive him to the railhead. They probably still talk about the incident in that town. Due to his illness, toward the end of 1966, Harry was spending more and more time away from the office. He'd stay for weeks at a time at his wife's home down in Mobile, Alabama.

That was the first box.

Another was the division of loyalties among the executives in our office into the Kroc people and the Sonneborn people. This situation was aggravated by a conflict between Harry and me over the appointment of executive vice-presidents. I had demanded that Fred Turner be made an executive vice-president. Harry's price for it was that Pete Crow be made one, too. Well, it was a dumb situation, but I had to go along with it. Dick Boylan was executive VP in charge of the budget and accounting; Pete Crow was head of new store development, which included real estate, construction, and licensing; and Fred Turner was in charge of the retail end, including operations, advertising and marketing, and equipment. Later on Fred took over licensing from Pete. Staffers referred to this three-headed setup as the "troika," and I never found anyone who was happy with it. The three executives were supposed to be equal in authority. The problem, however, was that Harry kept hold of the purse strings himself, and what the situation boiled down to, except with Boylan, was responsibility without authority.

Inside that box were several others having to do with Harry's direction of the company on a course that was completely opposite to the tack I wanted it to take. These ranged all the way from compensation for staffers to proposals that the arches be removed from new buildings. I approved taking them off, but as soon as Harry saw the plans, he'd say, "Put the goddam arches back!"

The most important problem I had with Harry, however, was his growing conservatism in real estate development. He was listening to bankers and others who told him the country was heading into a recession in 1967 and that McDonald's ought to conserve cash and hold down its construction of new stores.

Finally Harry put a moratorium on all new store development. No more construction. I was opposed to it, but when Luigi came into my office wringing his hands and complaining, I really couldn't give him any direction.

"Mr. Kroc, what am I going to do?" he asked. "I have thirty-three locations in the works. They are all good ones. We can't afford to lose them. What shall I do?"

"Tell 'em something vague, Luigi. String 'em along," I said. "I'm going to Chicago and see what I can do."

I was in our LaSalle Street offices the next morning waiting for Harry. When he came in we went at it hammer and tongs. I forced the issue all the way, with the result that he resigned. It was a hell of a mess, and I stewed about it all the way back to California.

I felt I needed legal advice, but I didn't want to go to Chapman & Cutler. They are a fine law firm, and I'm sure their opinion would have been honest and aboveboard. However, I thought that they were influenced too much by Harry, and I made up my mind that they wouldn't represent McDonald's in the future. So I called Don Lubin of Sonnenschein Carlin Nath & Rosenthal in Chicago and asked him to come out and talk to me. Don had done some personal legal work for me, and his firm had represented McDonald's in some matters early in our development.

Lubin's advice was that I try to patch it up with Harry. He knew that Harry was very close to the financial community, and he felt that a sudden resignation by this key individual seemed almost certain to hurt McDonald's. So I asked him to talk to Harry and try to get him to stay, although I really didn't think it was going to work. I also told Lubin that I wanted his firm to begin representing McDonald's, and I wanted him to go on our board of directors.

Harry agreed to stay, but it was an unhappy situation for both of us. He continued to spend more time in Alabama than he did in Chicago, and I felt he was just going through the motions of running the company. But it's true that his health was getting worse all the time. Finally we agreed he would resign. Based on his employment agreement, he would be paid $100,000 a year. Harry had a substantial chunk of McDonald's stock, but he was so certain the company would go down the chute when he left that he sold it all. He wanted the money, I'm told, to go into the banking business in Mobile. But it's a shame, because although the sale gave him a few million dollars at the time, the stock subsequently had a series of splits that made each share worth ten times as much. Had he kept it, his stock would be worth over $100 million. So his lack of faith in us was very costly for him.

I really had my work cut out for me now. I took the title of president and chairman of the board, and I removed that misguided moratorium on building new stores. In reviewing our real estate picture, I discovered all kinds of locations we had purchased and sort of stockpiled for future development. When I was told that we were waiting for the local economy to improve in those areas, I hit the ceiling.

"Hell's bells, when times are bad is when you want to build!" I screamed. "Why wait for things to pick up so everything will cost you more? If a location is good enough to buy, we want to build on it right away and be in there before the competition. Pump some money and activity into a town, and they'll remember you for it."

I also had to deal with the morale problem in our office. Much of the rift was healed as soon as Harry left. In fact, I heard one of our top execs quoted as saying, "Hooray, we're back in the hamburger business!" But we had been losing some good people as a result of the strained situation, and I didn't want to lose any more.

The guy I was chiefly concerned about was Fred Turner. He was extremely unhappy with his role in the "troika," and he had been sending out signals to indicate it. I knew that he had been getting a lot of telephone calls from other franchise operations. He'd had several very good offers for top positions. So before Harry's resignation was formally announced, I took Fred to dinner at the Whitehall.

"Fred, I know you have been unhappy lately," I told him. "I realize you have felt frustrated in your work. But I want to tell you something in complete confidence. Harry has resigned. I am going to take his title and do some fence mending and some ass kicking. This will take about a year. At the end of that year, I am going to make you president of McDonald's."

You could have toasted a McMuffin in the light of that smile of Fred's.

Then his face clouded, and his eyes bulged with anger. He hit the table with his fist so hard the silverware danced, and nearby diners flinched in alarm. "Dammit, if you knew about this frigged-up situation in the office, why didn't you do something about it?" he rasped.

For once in my life, I didn't answer fire with fire. I felt like a father who has failed to stick up for his son, and there was no way

I could explain to Fred the kind of tightrope I'd been on with Harry. So I told him to calm down, and one day he would figure it out for himself. Now I'm not so sure that's true, because Fred has no patience with office politics, and Harry's methods would be as foreign to him as they were to me. Anyhow, he couldn't stay mad for long. He was too happy. He said he was as glad about the resolution of the situation in the office as he was over being promised the presidency. I was relieved, because the rest of our conversation that evening showed that I had been a lot closer to losing Fred than I'd suspected.

A few of our executives left when Harry resigned, notably Pete Crow, who went back to his native Alabama to join a fast-fish chain called Catfish Hattie. But the thing we feared most—that a shattering loss of faith in McDonald's might run through the financial community when Harry departed—simply didn't happen. Dick Boylan moved right in behind Harry and kept the ball rolling for us with the bankers and the financial analysts. Dick had worked with these people all along, of course. Harry would initiate deals, but he left the detail work to Dick. So we had no problems. Office politicians and gossips had Dick figured as a Sonneborn man who would either quit when Harry left or when he himself didn't get the presidency. I knew Dick was above that though, and I think he understood that I would never appoint another president of McDonald's who didn't have a strong background in operations. So I pitched him the ball of chief financial officer, and he hit it over the grandstand.

Dick knew that I consider most of the language of high finance to be mumbo-jumbo. That bothered him, and he wanted to educate me a little bit. Also, he wanted to give the analysts the benefit of some of my sales message about McDonald's. Aloyis Sonneborn used to say I was the only guy she knew who could make a hamburger sound as appealing as filet mignon. I considered that a high compliment, because she is a woman of flawless good taste. Anyhow, Boylan started taking me to meetings with the analysts, and I enjoyed it. I came to appreciate their views a little more although I still think a lot of their approach is mumbo-jumbo. I also found that they really enjoyed straight talk about the nuts and bolts of our business.

My biggest task after Harry left the company was to recapture the territory we had granted back in our early and more innocent days to a pair of very smart business heads named John Gibson and Oscar Goldstein. They had an exclusive license like the one Lou Groen had for Cincinnati, but on a much grander scale. Their partnership, Gee-Gee Distributing Company, had the entire District of Columbia and a number of surrounding counties in Maryland and Virginia as an exclusive territory. We couldn't put up a single store in their area. Man-oh-man, that hurt!

Harry had done some dickering with Gibson and Goldstein in an effort to get the area back, but he wasn't willing to pay their price. This rubbed me the wrong way, because I knew we could develop that territory with substantially more than the forty-three stores Gee-Gee had there, and the real estate wasn't ever going to come down in price—no way!

I got my opportunity to corral the two big G's about five months after Harry left, when we met at our national operator's convention at the Doral Hotel in Miami Beach, Florida. They were hard bargainers. Goldstein had been a delicatessen owner in Washington, and Gibson had been an assistant secretary of labor in Truman's administration; so they knew which way the salami was sliced and who had the strongest hand in our negotiations: They did. But I managed to hammer out a deal for a few million dollars more than Harry Sonneborn had been willing to pay.

Gibson and Goldstein wound up getting about $16.5 million in cash. That was a very good dollar, but I didn't begrudge it. I don't stew about what the other guy is making in a deal like this; I'm concerned about whether it is going to be a good thing for McDonald's. Usually there's no reason both sides can't come out winners and be happy.

What we got in return was worth far more to McDonald's than the $16.5 million. We have increased the number of stores in the area from forty-three to ninety. But we also acquired a lot of fine executive talent in the move.

I had one personal reason for taking charge of the company myself after Harry Sonneborn left. We had recommended retail price increases to our operators for January 1967, and we weren't sure how badly the boost was going to affect us. I can still picture those newspaper headlines announcing, "The End of an Era: McDonald's 15-Cent Hamburger is Now 18 Cents." Whew! There had been a lot of controversy within the company about the increase. After all, it was our first, except for recommending raising cheeseburgers from nineteen cents to twenty cents and minor raises in fries, shakes, and Filet-O-Fish. After twelve years of operation, the fifteen-cent hamburger had come to be cherished as one of our foundation stones. Well, hell! We were in the midst of Lyndon Johnson's muddle-headed "guns *and* butter" economy with the war in Vietnam, and even our increasingly sophisticated purchasing operations could not cope with inflation. Some of our people believed we should recommend an increase to twenty cents instead of eighteen. But I came down hard on that one. They argued that customers wouldn't want to be bothered with pennies, and that it would be harder for our girls and boys to make change. However, if you look at it strictly from the customer's point of view—which is how I do it, because this guy is our real boss—you see the importance of every penny. And, cripes almighty, going to eighteen cents is a twenty percent increase! Anyhow, I prevailed. We made it eighteen cents, and then we waited anxiously for the sales figures and customer counts to come in so we could compare them to Gerry Newman's predictions. Gerry had drawn up an economic curve showing a diminishing demand for our product for every cent of increase in price. Past experience led us to expect an initial surge in volume as regular customers came in and paid the higher prices. This would be followed by a sharp drop as customers went to competitors. Then there would be a steady rise as the competition raised their prices and customers came back to us. That's exactly the pattern it followed. Volume increased twenty-two percent in January, followed by the worst February in many years. Our customer count dropped about nine percent. Would they come back? We were all confident they would, but I did not want to pass the baton to Fred Turner at that moment and make him come from behind. It took almost a year for our customer counts to recover. But 1967 ended very profitably, because the twenty percent price increase on twenty percent of our product added greatly to the income from our company stores. Of course, it didn't do our franchisees any harm either.

Another thing we had on the griddle and were watching closely throughout 1967 was our national advertising and marketing plan. This was being developed by Paul Schrage, who had worked on our account for D'Arcy Advertising in Chicago. Fred hired Paul to head our advertising and promotion department after he helped form the Operators National Advertising Fund (OPNAD), which allowed us to launch into national television. OPNAD is supported by a voluntary contribution of one percent of gross sales by licensees and company stores that belong to the program. Operators value highly the national advertising muscle that OPNAD gives them. What small businessman wouldn't cheerfully give up one percent of his gross to get our kind of commercials and things like sponsorship of *The Sound of Music* on network television to promote his store? He'd have to be crazy not to. In addition, operators contribute a percentage of their gross sales to an advertising co-operative in their local market. The co-ops retain their own area agencies and run their own campaigns, following guidelines established by the corporation.

I liked Paul Schrage's approach, because he was a "detail man" in his field, and he was on the same wave length as I was concerning the McDonald's image. For example, a great deal of study had gone into creating the appearance and personality of Ronald McDonald, right down to the color and texture of his wig. I loved Ronald. So did the kids. Even the sophisticates at *Esquire* magazine loved him. They invited Ronald to their "Party of the Decade" for top newsmakers of the sixties. McDonald's was chosen to cater the party because we had the "biggest impact on the eating out habits of Americans in the decade."

By early 1968 I was ready to hand the baton to Fred Turner, and he took it without breaking stride. As president and later chief executive officer, he pressed ahead with the programs I'd started and came up with some dynamic variations of his own. In a way, this was nepotism, because although I have never had a son, Fred is close to the age a boy of mine would have been, and he has all the desire and aptitude for the business that I could wish. So I've often said that I do have a son—his name is Fred Turner. He has never disappointed me. The great growth of the company over the last five years has been due to Fred's planning and vision and the work of Ed Schmitt and the rest of Fred's team of executives.

For openers he went gunning to recapture the Canadian market for McDonald's. Harry had made a deal just before he left the company to license most of western Canada to a man named George Tidball. The Ontario area was licensed to George Cohon, who had been an attorney in Chicago. Cohon's introduction to us was through a client who wanted to obtain a McDonald's license. George came to California to talk to me about it, and I was impressed by him. I told him, "Son, the best advice I can give you is to get out of law and into McDonald's. I think you've got what it takes." As it turned out, his client didn't get into McDonald's, but George did. Fred Turner had a high regard for George, too, but he didn't think he should have all that territory. Fred saw the Canadian market as being very similar to that in the United States, but with far less competition. So he set about buying back these big territorial licenses.

That was a pretty bold move. Stockholders might question the wisdom of licensing an area and then, two years later, buying it back for much more money. But Fred believed strongly in the potential of Canada, and he didn't let the possibility of adverse criticism slow him down. I thought, "That's my boy!"

McDonald's Canada is now one of our fastest growing and most lucrative markets. George Cohon is president of McDonald's of Canada, and his operators have the spirit of frontiersmen. They've achieved an average of a million dollars in sales for all their stores, which puts them well ahead of the United States.

There was one other thing I had to do to set the situation in the Chicago office straight, and that was to ask June Martino to retire. It was a tough thing for me. June was a wonderful person, and she had been a tremendous asset to the organization. But she was part of the old regime, and her approach would no longer work. June had the same deal Harry Sonneborn got. She held onto her stock, however, and it made her extremely wealthy.

I see June from time to time. She's an honorary director of the corporation, and she does some good work for McDonald's in the Palm Beach area. One thing June and I will always have in common is a love for McDonald's.

When I went back to California, I was looking forward to spending some time sitting in the sun instead of hammering away on the day-to-day direction of the company. I wanted to think

about the business less—maybe eighteen hours a day instead of
twenty-four—and I wanted to dream up future developments for
McDonald's. But a strange mood came over me when I got out
there. I was restless and even more irritable than usual. Maybe it
was a sort of premonition of the big change that was about to
occur in my life.

The western region operators had scheduled their convention in
San Diego, and they invited me to address them. Well, I thought,
sitting in the sun could wait till another time. This was a very
exciting period for McDonald's with a new president at the helm,
a couple of dynamite additions to our menu coming up in the Big
Mac and hot apple pie, a new style of architecture for our
buildings, new uniforms, and the opening of our beautiful new
campus for Hamburger U. in Elk Grove.

Damned right I'd talk to them! The more I thought about it, the
more excited I became at the prospect. There's nothing more fun
for me than rubbing elbows with a bunch of operators and talking
shop. But there was one couple listed on the advance registration
sheets that particularly interested me—the operators from Winne-
peg and Rapid City, South Dakota, Roland and Joni Smith.

14

I hadn't seen Joni for five years when we met at the Western Region Operators Convention in San Diego. Truthfully, I didn't expect to be hit by the same wave of emotion that had bowled me over before. But that's exactly what happened.

My suite in the hotel had a grand piano and a fireplace and bar. I brought Carl Eriksen along from the Los Angeles office to drive my new Rolls Royce and tend bar for parties in the suite. He hadn't bargained to be chaperone for Joni and me but, happily, that's the way it turned out. I attended a small dinner party the first evening of the convention, and Joni was there with her mother and Rollie. I made sure that Joni sat right next to me: "Rollie, you sit down there at the other end," I said. Everyone tittered. They thought I was kidding. Little did they know. And when I made my after-dinner speech about how I had attained all I'd ever wanted in life except one thing, little did they suspect that the missing element—all I needed to make life complete—was sitting there at that very table beside me. They probably thought I was referring to some staggering sales record or having Colonel Sanders become a McDonald's licensee or some such thing.

But Joni knew.

I knew she knew.

And she wasn't frowning. Man! I felt like a teenager on his first date. As I finished my little talk I could see that everyone was just going to get up from the table and depart—the evening was over. Well, not, by God, if I could help it!

"Come on, all of you," I announced. "We're going up to my suite and have some piano music and drinks."

They all came, including Joni and Rollie. He didn't stay long even though everyone was having a good time singing and laughing it up. Joni told him she was going to stay for a while. After a couple of hours, she and I were the last ones left except for Carl. He puttered around the place cleaning up and looking uncomfortable. I didn't want him to stay. But I wasn't prepared for the kind of stink it might cause if he left; so I told him to hang around. Joni and I talked and talked, and I lost all sense of time. I knew her husband would be madder than hell. But I didn't care, because Joan told me she was ready now to get a divorce regardless of what her family might say. She was ready at last to marry me, regardless of what gossips might say.

Beautiful!

Sleep was out of the question. Even after Joni left about four o'clock in the morning and Carl stretched out on the couch and was snoring like a buzz saw, I was spinning around like a top out of control. Then I remembered that I had to give the opening address to the convention that morning. I went into the bathroom and looked at myself in the mirror. Ouch! I put some eyewash in my eyes and took some Alka-Seltzer. Then some more eyewash. Then some aspirin. I couldn't remember what the hell I was going to say at the meeting.

Looking out from the rostrum at that huge crowd of operators as the meeting opened a couple of hours later, I still didn't know what I was going to say. All I could think of was that Joni and I had agreed that we would meet as soon as possible in Las Vegas, where we would get our separate divorces. I don't know what I said that morning, but I was told many times afterward that it was the most inspiring talk I ever gave.

Jane and I were supposed to be leaving on a world cruise. Joni had asked me to go through with it and break the news to Jane gently during the three months we would be gone. Okay. I thought I could handle that. But fond as I was of Jane, the more I thought about being away from Joni that long, the more impossible it became. First, I decided I would get off the boat in Hong Kong. Then I changed my mind and made it Acapulco. Then, by God, it was the Panama Canal. Finally, I said to hell with it, I would not go on the cruise at all.

I didn't want to hurt Jane any more than was necessary, but I had to have a divorce. Immediately! I took care, though, to insure that she would be financially secure. Jane still lives in our Beverly Hills home, and I continue to see some of her relatives who are long-time McDonald's operators.

I had bought a ranch in Southern California in 1965 with the intention of turning it into a center for McDonald's seminars and headquarters of the philanthropic foundation I had started the same year. It was a marvelous location, and I built a large lodge that had a spectacular view of the mountains surrounding it. Joni and I were married there, in front of the massive stone fireplace, on March 8, 1969.

At last I felt like a complete person. Now, I told myself, I could take life a little easier and enjoy it. I was finished grinding it out.

But business is not like painting a picture. You can't put a final brush stroke on it and then hang it on the wall and admire it. We have a slogan posted on the walls around McDonald's headquarters that says, "Nothing recedes like success. Don't let it happen to us or you." I wasn't about to let it happen to me. Fred Turner was doing a fine job of running the company, as I had known he would, but there were lots of areas that needed my attention.

In many corporations when the top guy moves up it's to a figurehead role. He becomes chairman of the bored. Not me. I admit that I no longer jump into the fray in administrative sessions and yell and pound on the table. That's for Fred and his executive staff. I'm content to sit back and listen and play Big Daddy, giving my opinion when it's asked. However, I am the chief guy when it comes to new product development and real estate acquisition. These are areas for which I have always had a special knack. I always enjoyed them most, so work is even more fun for me now than before I stepped up. I continue to look to the future of McDonald's and consider new menu items and new property in the light of overall corporate development. What I see in the future is unlimited possibilities for McDonald's—even more than existed for us ten years after I started the system. And now we have the talent and the financial resources to follow up on every business opportunity that presents itself. Fred has a top management team headed by Ed Schmitt, who became president and chief administrative officer in January 1977. He and his staff understand what makes the cash register ring and how to take care of the customer. That, of course, was always Fred Turner's strong suit as president. Fred has always been an operations man at heart. In January 1977, Fred was made chairman of the board. The board gave my chair another spin up to senior chairman. It is impossible to foresee what the new opportunities for McDonald's will be, but they are certain to come as the country grows and new social and economic needs take shape. Change has been our history, and you can't consider our growth without taking into account the context in which it occurred, an America in which tremendous social changes were taking place.

McDonald's is vastly different now from the company it was back in the early days, and that's good. We responded to the social changes of the late sixties by increasing minority hiring, and organizing a program to bring in qualified black and women operators. We've been a leader in advancing black capitalism. We also have made energy consumption in our stores more efficient than in the average home for preparing equivalent meals. We're international now. Hamburger U. has a handsome campus with classrooms equipped with the latest teaching aids. Our headquarters has its own modern, eight-story building in Oak Brook, a suburb west of Chicago. Jobs that one of us used to handle in a few minutes of spare time each week have grown into whole departments with hundreds of people on the staff.

Unfortunately, a few of our operators resented the changes. They couldn't see the big picture from the windows of their individual stores. Their operations hadn't changed, so why did the company have to change? They longed for the *good old days* when they could pick up the telephone and talk to Ray Kroc or Fred Turner to get help with their problems. As we became more

decentralized, those old-time operators found themselves responsible to district, regional, and zone executives who in many cases
were a lot newer to the organization than they were and who had
not lived through store openings with them as Fred Turner had or
helped them clean up their parking lots as I had. But there was
another element in the situation, and that was the fact that some
of these franchisees were approaching the end of their twenty-year
licenses. Among them was a handful of bad apples who knew
that their chances of being granted new franchises were slim.
These characters tried to gain company for their misery by
forming what they called the McDonald's Operators Association
(MOA). They organized in about 1973 and put out a newsletter
full of vicious gossip. Their theme quickly became trite—*The
company has changed. If you don't fight back you will be kicked out
when your franchise expires, and the company will take over the
store.* That's patent nonsense, because we don't want company-
owned stores to ever exceed more than about 30 percent of total
units. Moreover, we need good operators. It would be the height
of folly to kick out an operator who met our standards of quality,
service, and cleanliness, who had established his McDonald's in a
neighborhood, had built up good community relations and a
strong spirit among his employees. But MOA's whisper campaign
did stir up apprehensions. Even some of our good operators, who
should have known they had no need to worry, had to have
continual reassurances that we didn't intend to buy back their
stores. MOA was organized by Don Conley, an early corporation
employee, who instead of taking cheap shots at the company
should be saying a prayer of thanks to McDonald's every
morning. He was one of the small group who shared in the
purchase of Prince Castle Sales from me. But he put up no cash,
and all the payments on his note plus interest, which was only
about seven percent, were paid from dividends the group received
from Prince Castle's profits. When Prince Castle was sold to
Martin-Brower Corporation in less than two years, Conley made a
six-figure profit. He then acquired 20,000 shares of McDonald's
stock, which he's very smug and arrogant about today, since it
makes him a millionaire. How ironic that this came, in effect, as a
gift from me!

Conley is spiteful, perhaps, because he was fired. Anyhow,

June Martino felt sorry for Conley. She worked it so that he was able to buy two fine McDonald's stores—in lieu of severance pay, perhaps, since we had no real money in those days. At any rate, he got a sweetheart of a deal from us that he repaid with ingratitude.

We could have found what operators were involved in MOA and made it tough for them even though their membership lists were secret. But we didn't care to get involved in spying and intrigue. We refused to sink to their level. All we had to do was wait for their influence to evaporate. The good operators among them would eventually get disgusted with MOA's negativism. They would realize that while the corporation had grown large and, of necessity, more impersonal, our basic philosophy and our values had not changed.

> *Mental Snapshot:* I am sitting in Frank Cotter's office in 1954 discussing the licensing agreement he is drafting for me to use in the franchising arrangement I've set up with his clients, the McDonald brothers. He is insisting on all kinds of clauses and tortured phrases spelling out the relationship so that I will be able to "control" my licensees. I am getting sick as hell of his prissy niceties. I look out the window and ignore him until he finishes reading.
>
> "Listen, Frank," I tell him, "you can hogtie these guys with all the *ifs, buts,* and *whereases* you like, but it's not going to help the business one goddam bit. There'll be just one great motivator in developing loyalty in this operation. That is if I've got a fair, square deal, and the guy makes money. If he doesn't make money, I'm in a peck of trouble. I'm gonna lose my shirt. But I'll be right out there helping him and doing all I can to make sure he makes money. As long as I do that, I'll do just fine."

Back then, of course, I couldn't forsee an operator owning twenty-five or thirty stores. I couldn't envision situations in which an operator claimed we were hurting his sales volume by locating another store too close to his. I couldn't imagine having to deal with a franchise where an operator dies leaving his widow to run the store. (We have widows who are operators today, and they are good ones.) I wasn't thinking about what would happen when a franchise expired. But the basic philosophy of my statement to Cotter is as true today as it was then. We are an organization of small businessmen. As long as we give them a square deal and help them make money, we will be amply rewarded. I think that MOA has lost any power it ever had, and it will soon vanish. Fred made a fighting speech at our 1976 conventions in Florida and Hawaii, challenging them to come out in the open with any grievances they have or else get out of the way, because we are moving ahead—with them or without them. The silence since then can only mean that MOA is less.

With all these events clamoring to be dealt with, and government agencies such as OSHA making mountains of paperwork for us, some of the things I considered to be of major importance were going much too slowly. One of them was the new architectural look for our restaurants, the brick buildings with mansard roofs, stylish expanses of windows, and inside seating. It's worth noting that after this new style was adopted and had spread across the country it became the object of much serious discussion in architectural classes. James Volney Righter, who teaches architecture at Yale, says he believes the style "holds great potential in that it links the energy of lively American 'pop' forms with functional utility and quality construction. As the taste of the average consumer becomes more sophisticated, pressures are generated which might transform the visual and psychological energy of the American commercial strip into a cultural asset." He also talks about the "fascinating architectural problem of establishing an image easily identified by and desirable to the customer." I approved the new design in 1968, and it was to replace all of our red-and-white tile buildings. It was a drastic change in the image we'd established and in which we had a big investment, and Fred and I had to fight like hell to push it through the board of directors.

Brent Cameron, who is in charge of construction for us, is very conservative. Brent was the advocate of the MiniMac building, a scaled-down version of the new McDonald's restaurant that could be situated in smaller communities, where they might not have enough trade to support a full-sized store. This idea developed from a theory of Luigi Salveneschi's called "The Monotony Index." Luigi's idea was that the higher the level of monotony in a town, the better McDonald's chances of doing business there. "In big cities with all kinds of shops and restaurants, you are only one of thousands of choices," Luigi said. "But when you go into areas where there is nothing to do on Sunday afternoon, and people do not know how to spend their free time, your rate of frequency will go up dramatically. And there are literally thousands of areas like this where the *monotony index* is very high. These are people forgotten by industry and bypassed by superhighways and shopping centers. Yet they are important to us, the heart of America is still there in the boonies."

So Brent pushed the MiniMac concept. A booklet was published advancing it, and Fred Turner bought it.,

I was so damned mad I was ready to turn my office on the eighth floor of our new building into a batting cage and let those three guys have it with my cane. I had rheumatoid arthritis in my hip, and the pain of that didn't help my disposition any. But the reason I hated the MiniMac idea was that it was thinking small. Brent's plan was to buy enough property for a full-size store and put up a small unit. If it does well, then expand it. It was hard to argue against the program, because it took off very successfully. The initial MiniMac did about $70,000 gross the first month. But after they had built about twenty-two mini-units, some without seating and some with only thirty-eight seats, they finally got tired of my screaming and scrapped the program. And it's a damned good thing they did, because those minis were converted into regular stores and the majority of them are doing tremendous business. I believe that if you think small, you'll stay small.

Getting Brent turned around on the MiniMac program provided momentum for our remodeling and inside-seating campaign. I had to keep hammering away though, because in locations where I thought we needed 80 seats, they were putting in 50. Where I thought we needed 140, they were putting in 80.

You can argue both sides of this one. If you put in 140 seats, you may fill them for only an hour and a half at noon. The rest of the day you may have half of them empty. This is typical of a lot of restaurants in downtown locations. If you must cover a lot of empty seats for eighteen or twenty hours a day, the economics don't work out. But, of course, where McDonald's is concerned, I favor the high side. Fred Turner' does, too, and I like his thinking on it, which is that *business will expand to tax the facilities provided.* In other words, if you have a few extra feet of griddle and an extra fry station, or if you install one more cash register than existing business requires, you'll be challenged to put them to use.

While I'm talking about Brent Cameron, I should point out that I've always considered our conflicts creative. We first started butting heads in California, when he was an area supervisor in Los Angeles. He and Fred usually take the conservative stand on any issue. I'm the liberal, and that always makes for interesting executive meetings.

Some of my detractors, and I've acquired a few over the years, say that my penchant for experimenting with new menu items is a foolish indulgence. They contend that it stems from my never having outgrown my drummer's desire to have something new to sell. "McDonald's is in the hamburger business," they say. "How can Kroc even consider serving chicken?" Or, "Why change a winning combination?"

Of course, it's not difficult to demonstrate how much our menu has changed over the years, and nobody could argue with the success of additions such as the Filet-O-Fish, the Big Mac, Hot Apple Pie, and Egg McMuffin. The most interesting thing to me about these items is that each evolved from an idea of one of our operators. So the company has benefited from the ingenuity of its small businessmen while they were being helped by the system's image and our cooperative advertising muscle. This, to my way of thinking, is the perfect example of capitalism in action. Competition was the catalyst for each of the new items. Lou Groen came up with Filet-O-Fish to help him in his battle against the Big Boy chain in the Catholic parishes of Cincinnati. The Big Mac resulted from our need for a larger sandwich to compete against Burger King and a variety of specialty shop concoctions. The idea for Big Mac was originated by Jim Delligatti in Pittsburgh. Harold Rosen, our operator in Enfield, Connecticut, invented our special St. Patrick's Day drink, The Shamrock Shake. "It takes a guy with a name like *Rosen* to think up an Irish drink," Harold told me. He wasn't kidding. "You may be right," I said. "It takes a guy with a name like Kroc to come up with a Hawaiian sandwich ... Hulaburger." He didn't say anything. He didn't know whether I was kidding or not. Operators aren't the only ones who come up with creative ideas for our menu. My old friend Dave Wallerstein, who was head of the Balaban & Katz movie chain and has a great flair for merchandising—he's the man who put the original snack bars in Disneyland for Walt Disney—is an outside director of McDonald's, and he's the one who came up with the idea for our large size order of french fries. He said he loved the fries, but the small bag wasn't enough and he didn't want to buy two. So we kicked it around and he finally talked us into testing the larger size in a store near his home in Chicago. They have a window in that store that they now call "The Wallerstein Window," because every time the manager or a crew person would look up, there would be Dave peering in to see how the large size fries were selling. He needn't have worried. The large order took off like a rocket, and it's now one of our best-selling items. Dave really puts his heart into his job as a director, now that he's retired and has plenty of time. There's nothing he likes more than traveling with me to check out stores.

Our Hot Apple Pie came after a long search for a McDonald's kind of dessert. I felt we had to have a dessert to round out our menu. But finding a dessert item that would fit readily into our production system and gain wide acceptance was a problem. I thought I had the answer in a strawberry shortcake. But it sold well for only a short time and then slowed to nothing. I had high hopes for pound cake, too, but it lacked glamor. We needed something we could romance in advertising. I was ready to give up when Litton Cochran suggested we try fried pie, which he said is an old southern favorite. The rest, of course, is fast-food history. Hot Apple Pie, and later Hot Cherry Pie, has that special quality, that classiness in a finger food, that made it perfect for McDonald's. The pies added significantly to our sales and revenues. They also created a whole new industry for producing the filled, frozen shells and supplying them to our stores.

During the Christmas holidays in 1972, I happened to be visiting in Santa Barbara, and I got a call from Herb Peterson, our operator there, who said he had something to show me. He wouldn't give me a clue as to what it was. He didn't want me to reject it out of hand, which I might have done, because it was a crazy idea—a breakfast sandwich. It consisted of an egg that had been formed in a Teflon circle, with the yolk broken, and was dressed with a slice of cheese and a slice of grilled Canadian bacon. This was served open-face on a toasted and buttered English muffin. I boggled a bit at the presentation. But then I tasted it, and I was sold. Wow! I wanted to put this item into all of our stores immediately. Realistically, of course, that was impossible. It took us nearly three years to get the egg sandwich fully integrated into our system. Fred Turner's wife, Patty, came up with the name that helped make it an immediate hit—Egg McMuffin.

The advent of Egg McMuffin opened up a whole new area of potential business for McDonald's, the breakfast trade. We went after it like the Sixth Fleet going into action. It was exhilarating to see the combined forces of our research and development people, our marketing and advertising experts, and our operations and supply specialists all concentrating on creating a program for catering to the breakfast trade. There were a great many problems to overcome. Some of them were new to us, because we were dealing with new kinds of products. Pancakes, for example, have to be offered if you intend to promote a complete breakfast menu. But they have an extremely short holding time, and this forced us to devise a procedure for "cooking to order" during periods of low customer count. Our food assembly lines, so swift and efficient for turning out hamburgers and french fries, had to be geared down and realigned to produce items for the breakfast trade. Then, after all the planning and all the working out of supply and production problems, it remained for the individual operator to figure out whether to adopt breakfast in his store. It meant longer hours for him, of course, and he'd probably have to hire more crew members and give the ones he had additional training. Consequently, the breakfast program is growing at a very moderate rate. But I can see it catching on across the country, and I can visualize extensions for a lot of stores, such as brunch on Sunday.

I keep a number of experimental menu additions in the works all the time. Some of them now being tested in selected stores may find their way into general use. Others, for a variety of reasons, will never make it. We have a complete test kitchen and experimental lab on my ranch, where all of our products are tested; this is in addition to the creative facility in Oak Brook. Fred Turner has a tendency to look askance at any new menu ideas. He'll usually try to put them down with some wisecrack such as, "That may be all right, but when are we going to start serving grilled bananas? We could put a little container of maple syrup on the side, and maybe for dinner we could serve them flaming." Such sarcasm doesn't bother me. I know Fred's thinking, and I respect it. He doesn't want us going hog wild with new items. We aren't going to, but we are going to stay flexible and change as the market demands it. There are some things we can do and maintain our identity, and there are others we could never do. For example, it's entirely possible that one day we might have pizza. On the other hand, there's damned good reason we should never have hot dogs. There's no telling what's inside a hot dog's skin, and our standard of quality just wouldn't permit that kind of item.

Some executives have maps of the country with different colored pins indicating their sales outlets. I don't have such a map. I don't need one, because I have it all in my mind, and that includes the kind of store on a given location, who the operator is, what kind of volume he's doing, what his problems are, and so forth. Of course, with 4,000 locations to keep in mind, I can't keep as current on every store's operations as a franchisee's field consultant or his district manager. But I keep in touch through my real estate activities.

Back in the days when we first got a company airplane, we used to spot good locations for McDonald's stores by flying over a community and looking for schools and church steeples. After we got a general picture from the air, we'd follow up with a site survey. Now we use a helicopter, and it's ideal. Scarcely a month goes by that I don't get reports from whatever districts happen to be using our five copters on some new locations that we would never have discovered otherwise. We have a computer in Oak Brook that is designed to make real estate surveys. But those printouts are of no use to me. After we find a promising location, I drive around it in a car, go into the corner saloon and into the neighborhood supermarket. I mingle with the people and observe their comings and goings. That tells me what I need to know about how a McDonald's store would do there. Hell, if I listened to the computers and did what they proposed with McDonald's, I'd have a store with a row of vending machines in it. You'd push some buttons and out would come your Big Mac, shake, and fries, all prepared automatically. We could do that; I'm sure Jim Schindler could work it out. But we never will. McDonald's is a *people* business, and the smile on that counter girl's face when she takes your order is a vital part of our image.

Finding locations for McDonald's is the most creatively fulfilling thing I can imagine. I go out and check out a piece of property. It's nothing but bare ground, not producing a damned thing for anybody. I put a building on it, and the operator gets into business there employing fifty or a hundred people, and there is new business for the garbage man, the landscape man, and the people who sell the meat and buns and potatoes and other things. So out of that bare piece of ground comes a store that does, say, a million dollars a year in business. Let me tell you, it's a great satisfaction to see that happen.

In 1974 The Fourteen Research Corporation published a seventy-five-page analysis of McDonald's growth projected through 1999. It described very neatly our financial position and the kind of real estate development I myself foresee:

> The basis of McDonald's success is serving a low-priced, value-oriented product fast and efficiently in clean and pleasant surroundings. While the company's menu is limited, it contains food staples that are widely accepted in North America. It is for these reasons that demand for its products is less sensitive to economic fluctuations than most other restaurant formats.

> Until the early 1970s, McDonald's was expanding almost

exclusively in the suburbs. Yet for quite a while it had been spending a great deal on national advertising that was creating a latent, nationwide demand for its product. Thus, the stage was set for the company to diversify and strengthen its expansion program. There are now over 100 stores located in cities, shopping centers, and even on college campuses; most are doing exceptionally well, with many more planned.

We firmly believe that McDonald's can successfully locate a store almost anywhere there are primary concentrations of population (i.e., suburbs and cities) and secondary concentrations (schools, shopping centers, industrial parks, stadiums, etc.) provided that capital turnover rates meet corporate objectives. It is this "nook and cranny" type of expansion along with continued conventional growth that leads us to project that on average 485 new stores will be added each year (through 1979) to world operations.

Nook and cranny expansion. Exactly! There are countless nooks and crannies throughout the country that are possible locations for us, and we fully intend to expand into them.

What does it take to get a McDonald's franchise? A total commitment of personal time and energy is the most important thing. A person doesn't need to be super smart or have more than a high school education, but he or she must be willing to work hard and concentrate exclusively on the challenge of operating that store. The value of our franchises has increased greatly over the years. I started issuing them for $950 back in 1955. Ten years later, when we went public, the average investment was $81,500. These days it takes about $200,000 for the franchise and related expenses—equipment, furnishings, signs, etc.—not counting interest or finance charges on borrowed money.

In the initial interview, the applicant is told what we expect and what the corporation will contribute. If he's still interested after learning about the kind of personal and financial investment required, we put him to work in a McDonald's store near his home. He's assigned to evening or weekend hours that won't conflict with his present job, and he learns firsthand what's involved in both crew work and management. If he's not really suited for our kind of restaurant operation, this is the time to find that out. After this experience and a final discussion with the licensing manager in his area, the applicant puts up his $4,000 deposit and is informed of the market area in which his restaurant is likely to be located. We never promise a specific community. Getting onto the list of registered applicants waiting for a location is harder than it used to be, because we give preference to present operators and to McDonald's employees who have been with the corporation for ten years or more.

The applicant is advised when a site comes up for him (usually less than two years after his registration), and if he's still interested after looking over the location, we begin getting him more involved in McDonald's. We stay in close contact as he arranges to join us, divesting himself of another business, perhaps, selling a home, and looking for a new one in the community where his store is to be located. We now ask him to spend another 500 hours working in a McDonald's restaurant. He's also invited to attend orientation and management classes. Then, about four to six months prior to the date his store is scheduled to open, the licensee attends our advanced operations course at Hamburger U. This adds polish to the management skills and operations know-how he'll need to greet his first customers.

All of this preparatory work and training helps insure success for the small businessman who gets a McDonald's franchise. And it doesn't stop there. We stay right in there helping him through our system of field representatives.

It's all interrelated—our development of the restaurant, the training, the marketing advice, the product development, the research that has gone into each element of our equipment package. Together with our national advertising and continuing supervisory assistance, it forms an invaluable support system. Individual operators pay 11.5 percent of their gross to the corporation for all of this, and I think it's a hell of a bargain.

Art Bender, my first franchisee, says he's sometimes asked why he doesn't just start his own restaurant instead of paying a percentage of his gross to McDonald's. After all, he helped teach Ray Kroc the business; he could make it on his own easily.

"I might have a successful restaurant," Art says, "but I'd hate to think what it would cost me as an individual to buy the services I get from the corporation. The name itself is worth a lot, of course. National advertising with Art's Place? No way. Then there's purchasing power, Hamburger U. training for my managers, product development . . . how could I do all that alone?"

Our development in urban areas has been challenging, because it represents an entirely different kind of real estate situation. There also are all kinds of social and political currents swirling around in a big city that you don't have to deal with in suburbia. Occasionally activists of one kind or another have tried to use an attack on McDonald's to advance whatever cause they were pushing. We are a convenient symbol of establishment business. Our development in New York City, for example, was characterized by snobbish writers as some sort of sinister plot. Here was Daddy Warbucks dressed up like Ronald McDonald setting out to milk money from an unsuspecting populace. What these fanatics actually opposed was the capitalist system. Their political cant held that to be successful in the context of free enterprise, a business must be morally corrupt and guilty of all kinds of shabby business practices. I feel sorry for people who have such a small and wretched view of the system that made this country great. Fortunately, their hysterics rarely make much of an impression on residents, who welcome the clean and wholesome kind of operation McDonald's runs. They realize that our stores can help upgrade their community. There are rare circumstances in which a neighborhood genuinely feels that McDonald's would not be in keeping with its character. This happened in the posh Lexington Avenue area of New York City, and we withdrew. It cost us a lot of money, but we sure don't want to locate in an area where people don't want us—that makes for a losing business proposition. But if any of the aristocratic residents of Lexington Avenue think McDonald's can't be a tasteful, refined, and socially uplifting operation, a visit to Water Tower Place in Chicago might change their minds. Our neighbors in this ultramodern Michigan Avenue building include the classiest names in retailing. Our store there does a tremendous business, even though we have to explain to an occasional mink-furred dowager that, like it or not, she has to go to the counter and order her own hamburger, we have no table service.

It was wonderful to see all these changes taking place in McDonald's and to be part of them. However, I was finding it increasingly difficult to keep up. Some days I could hardly get around because of the way arthritis was warping my hip. Yet pain was preferable to idleness, and I kept moving despite Joni's urging that we settle down on our ranch. She really loves it there. So do I. But there were a lot of things I wanted to do that could not be accomplished from an easy chair.

For one, I wanted to own the Chicago Cubs, the baseball team I had been rooting for since I was seven years old. In 1972 the time seemed ripe and I tried to make an offer, but Phil Wrigley wouldn't even talk to me. He sent word that if the club was for sale, I was the sort of person he would like to have buy it—but it wasn't for sale. That made me madder than hell, because Wrigley is just sitting on that team. He hasn't done a damn thing to improve them, but he won't give them up and let someone else do it. It's idiotic. The message he sent me indicated that he might change his mind one of these days, but I sure as hell wasn't going to sit around waiting for that to happen. I just forgot about the whole thing. I wasn't even considering going into baseball when I was flying out to Los Angeles to meet Joni early in 1974 and read the sports stories about the impending sale of the San Diego Padres. I thought to myself, "My God, San Diego is a gorgeous town. Why don't I go over there and look at that ball park?" I've always admired Buzzy Bavasi, who was running the team, and the whole thing sounded very appealing. So I got in the car with Joni at the airport and told her that I was thinking of buying the San Diego Padres. She looked at me quizzically and said, "What on earth is that, a monastery?"

15

Everyone, including my wife and the commissioner of baseball, was shocked when I grabbed the public address microphone at the Padre's first home game in 1974 and chewed out the players for putting on a rotten performance. The 40,000 fans roared, and the baseball writers went crazy. Joni was on the telephone as soon as I got back to the hotel to say she was ashamed of me. How could I do such a thing? Was I drunk? No, I assured her, I wasn't drunk. I was just plain mad as hell.

That moment had been building for a good many weeks, probably since I first asked Don Lubin to begin negotiations to buy the team for me. I had read that the owner, California banker C. Arnholt Smith, was in deep financial difficulty and would be forced to sell. Several groups had expressed interest, so there was more than a little suspense about the affair. Don called Buzzy Bavasi, general manager of the club, and told him that Ray Kroc wanted to buy.

"That's fine," Buzzy said. "Who else is in the group?"

"He *is* the group." There was a long, skeptical silence. Then Don added, "He owns seven million shares of McDonald's common stock, which is selling for about fifty-five dollars a share." Buzzy did a little mental arithmetic and said he would be glad to talk to Mr. Smith about it.

We had a preliminary meeting in which I swapped baseball yarns with Buzzy and his son, Peter. We hit it off right from the start. I'd always admired Buzzy and respected his professionalism since the days when he was one of the old Brooklyn Dodgers and was associated with baseball executives like Larry MacPhail, Branch Rickey, and Walter O'Malley. Our chat stirred all the memories of my lifelong interest in baseball and made me set my heart on owning this team. But there were to be many anxious weeks of bargaining before the deal was concluded. Smith at first wanted half a million dollars more than I was willing to pay. After the price was agreed upon, his lawyers still stalled while trying to extricate him from his problems with the government. Don Lubin kept me posted by telephone on the day to day meetings with the Smith group. In one crucial session, held in an elegant suite atop a bank that Smith had once controlled, the going got particularly heavy, and Don and his partner, Bob Grant, held a strategy conference in a room that looked out over San Diego Bay. He told me later that they believed Smith was ready to throw in the towel and go along with our demands, but they weren't sure. Then they noticed a photograph on a table that was so faded by the sun they could barely make out the faces of the three men in it—C. Arnholt Smith, Richard M. Nixon, and Spiro Agnew. That symbol of faded glory was particularly striking in the wake of Watergate, and it gave my men a psychic lift—they went to bat with renewed vigor. Finally, they narrowed the differences down to one or two points. I flew into San Diego late one evening and met with them and Smith.

"Look, Mr. Smith, we have delayed long enough," I said. "Unless this deal is signed now, there isn't going to be any deal."

We signed.

The Padres had been in the cellar for five straight years, so I wasn't expecting any miracles. I told the sportswriters I thought it would take at least three years to build the team up, and I wasn't surprised when they started the season by dropping a three-game series in Los Angeles. Disappointed but not surprised.

I was greeted like a hero in San Diego. Old men and little boys stopped me in the street to thank me for saving baseball for the city. The mayor presented me with an award in the opening ceremonies of our first home game. The sportswriters also gave me an award, the U.S. Navy Band and Marine Band played, and cameras flashed as I stood there, arms raised, making the V-sign, acknowledging the cheers like a Presidential candidate.

Gordon McRae sang the national anthem and the umpire called, "Play ball!" I was so excited when that first Houston Astro batter walked to the plate that I could hardly contain myself. But the mood passed quickly as I watched error after error by my team. After a few innings I got disgusted.

Then the Padres showed some signs of life. They loaded the bases with one out. Our fourth batter hit a high pop-up behind the plate, and we all watched it tensely, giving it body English, trying to will it to fall into the stands for a foul strike. But the Houston catcher took it for the second out. I turned to Don Lubin and said, "Doggone it. We had a rally going there. Well, we still have one out left."

As I turned to watch the play again I was astonished to see the Astros trotting in off the field. "What's the matter?" I yelled. "There's still one out to go!" Don shook his head and said, "Yes, there was. But our man on first ran to second on that foul fly and was doubled off first by the catcher."

That really made me furious. I jumped up and stomped down to the PA booth. The man at the microphone looked up in disbelief as I burst in. "Hello, Mr. Kroc," he said. Without replying, I grabbed the microphone out of his hands. At that very instant a man ran stark naked across the playing field from the left field stands. My voice boomed out into every corner of the park, "Get that streaker out of here! Arrest him! Get the police!" The streaker was never caught, but he had created quite a stir in the audience. It was nothing, however, compared to the commotion I was about to generate.

"This is Ray Kroc speaking," I told the fans. I said I had good news and bad news for them. There were ten thousand more of them in the park that evening than had turned out to see the Los Angeles Dodgers' opener in the larger Chavez Ravine stadium a few nights before. That was the good news. "The bad news is that we are putting on a lousy show for you," I bellowed. "I apologize for it. I'm disgusted with it. This is the most stupid baseball playing I've ever seen!"

Interviewers still ask me about that incident. Usually the question is whether I regret it. The answer is *hell no!* I only regret that I didn't lay it on them a lot harder. I did have to make a diplomatic apology to the commissioner, but I have the satisfaction of being responsible for a new rule in baseball—no one but the official announcer can use the public address system at a game. I also introduced a novel concern to baseball. It was my insistence, well known to McDonald's employees, that customers receive a quality product for their money. Apparently I was the first owner ever to suggest that players owe top performance to the fans who support them.

At the time, reaction to my outburst was mixed. Newspaper columnists expounded on it, and television commentators hashed it over. I think that, generally, they agreed with the point I was making—that it's no crime to lose unless you fail to do your best. All kinds of baseball personalities were quoted pro and con as to how that applies to professional players. Doug Rader, the third baseman for the Houston Astros (who later joined our club), said, "Who the hell does he think he's talking to, a bunch of short order cooks?" I told the press that Rader had insulted all short order cooks, and I invited any of them in the San Diego area to be my guests at the opening game of our next home series against the Astros. If they came wearing a chef's hat, they would be admitted to the ball park free. Thousands of people showed up in chef's hats for that game, and they were all seated behind third base. Rader was presented with a chef's hat at home plate before the game started. Our fans booed every play he made during the game—all in the spirit of fun, of course.

It was wonderful to see how the San Diego fans got behind the Padres and supported them even when they were losing, which was most of the time during our first two seasons. Attendance at the park has increased dramatically each year. It will get even better as the team continues to improve. We have had a lot of fun encouraging this spirit with promotions like tailgate parties, which had become traditional for football games and adapted readily to baseball. One time I gave away ten thousand dollars in a big money-grab before the game. We picked forty spectators out of the stadium at random and let them onto the field, which was strewn with paper money. They could keep all they could pick up in a certain time limit, and I'll tell you, there was some mighty scrambling out there.

Buzzy clearly appreciates my active interest in the team. All too many owners are absentee landlords, he says. We stay in touch by telephone all the time. When he first took me on a tour to meet the office staff, I was appalled at the wages we were paying. I understood that had been necessary because of Smith's financial troubles, but I didn't want the front office folks to think I was a miser. I'm not talking about players; they're pros and have good contracts. I told Buzzy, "I want you to give all these people raises, across the board." He really boggled at that. He told me that baseball people traditionally scrimp by on very low pay. They have to, because they have more bad years than good years. I replied that, tradition be damned, any team I own is going to pay decent wages. Well, we compromised on it. We didn't make an across-the-board increase. But I made sure that the people who deserved a raise got one. They all got bonuses at Christmas and when the team was doing well. Buzzy had to admit later that part of the team's increasing success is due to the new interest and efficiency in our front office.

Our ball park is owned by the City of San Diego, so I can't do as I please there. Some of my plans for landscaping and other improvements to beautify the park got scuttled by the city fathers. No hard feelings. They have their football crowds to consider, and my plans would have eliminated some seating. But I keep coming up with ideas to make our games a more pleasant experience. One of them was the electric one-man-band, a player piano rigged up with drums and cymbals and all kinds of other effects. I had it painted Padres yellow and brown and installed it near the entrance to the stadium. Buzzy thought it was really a nutty idea. But he changed his tune when he saw how the crowds gather around to watch it play before games. I also came up with the idea for selling a big bucket of popcorn for a dollar. We promoted it as *the world's biggest box of popcorn.* I have some other ideas along this line, too, such as the new kind of cookie we're calling the *Farkelberry Snickerdoodle*—I got the idea from Jim Delligatti in Pittsburgh, where Snickerdoodles have been described as "albino brownies with measles." I am just getting started with these promotions.

The team itself is improving all the time. Before the start of the 1977 season we added some fine players in Gene Tenace, a catcher, fielder, and power hitter, and Rollie Fingers, an outstanding relief pitcher, both of whom were formerly with the Oakland A's. Another relief pitcher, Butch Metzger, was named Rookie of the Year for the 1976 season. We were expecting another super season from pitcher Randy Jones, a regular starter who won the Cy Young Award in 1976.

On the whole, owning the Padres has been very rewarding. One of the best things about it was discovering the progressive spirit of San Diego. I think it's destined to become one of the fastest-growing communities in the country. It's wonderful. Weather conditions are perfect for all kinds of manufacturing, labor is plentiful, and there's an energetic mood about the place that Phoenix and Miami and Fort Lauderdale once had but have lost. That's why I bought the San Diego Mariners of the World Hockey League in August 1976. I felt the city deserved to have professional hockey as well as baseball and football. The team had been popular but was losing money. It needed some strong business direction, and I think Buzzy and I and my son-in-law, Ballard Smith, who is vice-president and general manager of the team, can give it that. Personally, I've never paid much attention to hockey. But I know that it's fast and colorful, and I'm told that after you see a couple of games you get hooked. We'll see. . . .

Doing things like buying baseball teams and hockey teams always opens a person to criticism from folks who think they have better ideas about how one's money should be spent. There is a common fallacy that money will solve problems. It won't. Money creates problems, and the more you have, the bigger the problems, not the least of which is how to spend it wisely.

People have sometimes accused me of being a hungry tiger for money. That's not true. I've never done anything for the sake of money alone. Several years ago, when we were first beginning to generate big income, I made a speech at a financial meeting, and a fellow got up and said, "Isn't it interesting that Mr. Kroc has so much enthusiasm and spirit. You know that he owns four million McDonald's shares and the stock went up five dollars." I was floored. Actually embarrassed. The fellow was looking at me. So I said into the mike, "So what! I can still only wear one pair of shoes at a time." I got a hell of a hand. But, you see, that's the mentality. The person who thinks only in terms of "Where's mine?" can't imagine anyone else not thinking the same way. We've actually had writers criticize McDonald's policy of furnishing free coffee and hamburgers when natural disasters strike as being a self-serving public relations gimmick. That's kind of hard to take, because we're always trying to be good neighbors and responsible citizens. We've always encouraged our franchisees to become involved in community activities and to make donations to worthwhile charities.

Other unfair things have been published about us. For example, we were accused of having torn down a Greek Revival "landmark" building in Cambridge, Massachusetts, so we could build a McDonald's on the site. The writers failed to mention that the building was a wreck. It had been vandalized and burned before we bought it. The city of Cambridge had refused to designate it as a landmark building. That store had a rough time after it opened in 1974 because of all the politically motivated demonstrations against it. The operator, Lawrence Kimmelman, was only able to hang on because he had a couple of other stores in the Boston area. Gradually, however, the residents of Cambridge began to realize that the store was an asset to them. They forgot about all the negative rhetoric. Business picked up. A black woman who was a Democratic ward coordinator and had been one of the most vocal opponents of our opening was so impressed later that she went to work for Kimmelman in that store. Then in 1976 Congressman and Speaker of the House Thomas P. "Tip" O'Neill told Kimmelman he was glad that McDonald's had overcome their problems in Cambridge because, "You are doing a terrific job of community service here."

We were accused of "shocking manipulation" in our dispute with labor unions in San Francisco. I suppose that's another way of saying we don't fool around. It's always shocking to be a loser. I was quoted as asking Mayor Alioto, "What would it take to put a third McDonald's in San Francisco?" I never spoke those words or any like them.

None of this is meant to sound as though I think I've never made a mistake. Far from it. I could probably write another book about my mistakes. But it wouldn't be very interesting. I've never seen negatives add up to a plus.

One time Harry Sonneborn, June Martino, and I invested in a beer garden restaurant on the south side of Chicago. That was a loser. I tried my hand with an idea for an elegant hamburger restaurant called Ramond's. The corporation opened two of them, one in Beverly Hills, the other in Chicago. They didn't take hold, so I cut our losses and got out. One good thing came of Ramond's: it gave us the prototype for the in-city McDonald's restaurants that are now proving so popular. Part of the problem with Ramond's was my insistence on quality in a restricted-volume kind of operation, which kept the profit margin thin as the skin on a hot dog. The same was true of a venture we started back in my California days, the Jane Dobbins Pie Tree chain. Hell of an idea. Great pies, too. In fact, they were so good we were going broke selling them. I've also come up with some pretty big flops for McDonald's. I've already done the blow-by-blow on the ill-fated Hulaburger and told how it was devoured by the voracious Filet-O-Fish. Lou Groen still ribs me about that if he gets a chance. Roast beef was another bust. We were pretty excited about it at first. But roast beef is difficult for our kind of operation to deal with. It went well in a few stores, but it simply did not adapt to our system. We learned a lot about testing requirements in that roast beef fiasco, though. That's important, because if you are willing to take big risks, and I always have been, you are bound to blow one once in a while; so when you strike out, you should try to learn as much as you can from it. I think we probably found out enough about our own methods from the roast beef experiment to more than make up what we lost on it.

There's one other mistake I made that I mention only because so many jackasses have brayed about it. That was my $250,000 donation to President Nixon's campaign in 1972. I let myself be talked into that by Nixon's fund raiser, Maurice Stans, and it wasn't until later that I realized I had made the contribution for the wrong reason. My motive was not so much pro-Nixon as it was anti-George McGovern. I should have known at the time that this went against my rule of not trying to make a positive out of a negative action. The worst thing about the donation was the subsequent implication by some sons of bitches that I had made it in order to get favorable treatment from the federal price commission in regard to the price of our Quarter Pounder. As my friend and lawyer, Fred Lane, says, "This has been thoroughly investigated by the Watergate Select Committee, the Government Accounting Office, the Department of Justice, and the House Committee on Impeachment, and none found any hint of impropriety." I use his language because my own is unprintable.

A student at one of my talks at Dartmouth asked if I demanded that my executives in McDonald's follow my politics.

"I can answer that," Fred Turner interjected. "Kroc voted for Nixon and I voted for McGovern."

"That's right," I added, "and we were both wrong."

After the laughter died down, I added, "I believe that if two executives think the same, one of them is superfluous."

I get as mad as hell and cuss when someone takes cheap shots at McDonald's or me in print. Yet I always admired Harry Truman and liked what he said about getting out of the kitchen if you can't stand the heat. I'm not about to get out of the kitchen. I've got a lot more plans I want to carry out for McDonald's before I hang up my spatula.

16

One evening not long after I had bought the San Diego Padres I was shooting the bull with Dave Condon, sports columnist for the *Chicago Tribune*. We got onto the subject of that great Cubs team of 1929, when they made it to the World Series against Philadelphia. "You know, Dave," I told him, "I am the perfect example of reincarnation. I died the day Hack Wilson lost that fly ball in the sun!"

Kidding aside, I do sometimes feel as if I've been given an extra shot at life. I owe this to medical science, and that's why I set up the Kroc Foundation.

I had resisted the foundation proposal at first because it was presented as a tax shelter. I'm not interested in that sort of thing. I don't make charitable donations because they will give me tax deductions. That's a peculiarity of mine that runs against common business practice. It's the same thing with expense accounts. I've never submitted a personal expense account to McDonald's in my life. In the early days, of course, it would have been an empty exercise. I didn't take a salary; I was keeping the thing afloat with my income from Prince Castle Sales. But even in later years it never entered my mind that I should be reimbursed by the company. I pay most of my company expenses out of my own pocket, although, of course, I do use my company credit card. By the same token, I have purchased a fleet of nineteen customized Greyhound buses, outfitted with kitchens, rest rooms, telephones, color television, and lounge-style seating and I rent these to the corporation for one dollar a year. Each of our districts books the use of one of these Big Mac buses to its operators for worthwhile activities such as taking disadvantaged children and senior citizens on outings. I also bought the company plane, a Grumman Gulfstream G-2 jet. McDonald's rents it from me for the same low price, one dollar a year. The G-2 can fly anywhere in the world, and we make good, cost-cutting use of it for executive travel. My point here is that I believe in spending my money in useful ways. It wasn't until Don Lubin proposed the foundation as a means to benefit medical research that I pricked up my ears and started paying attention.

As we discussed the idea, I realized that my brother would be exactly the right man to make president of the foundation. Robert L. Kroc is a Ph.D., and in 1965 he was head of the physiology department in the research institute of Warner-Lambert, the pharmaceutical firm. His specialty was endocrinology, and he was widely respected in the field. It was not easy to persuade Bob to give up his post and his home in Morristown, New Jersey, and move his household to my ranch in Southern California. But he finally did it in 1969, and he has done a fine job of establishing the foundation. The headquarters building at the ranch has complete facilities for scientific conferences and presentation of research papers.

My brother Bob talks the language of science. He's pedantic and painstaking; he's willing to get fewer things done in order to make fewer mistakes. I'm impatient. I'm willing to make a few mistakes in order to get things done. So our thinking is miles apart on the handling of money for the foundation. I never realized it could be so damned difficult to give away money. Our grants seem to take endless study and deliberation. Yet I must say that Bob has managed to fund some important research. We have had many highly esteemed scientists and physicians attend our conferences, and the results of their sessions have been published as books and as supplements to the most prestigious medical journals.

The Kroc Foundation supports research into diabetes, arthritis, and multiple sclerosis. All three of these diseases strike young adults and rob them of vitality in their best years. I selected them for that reason, and also because each has touched my own life destructively. I have diabetes myself. My first wife, who is now dead, suffered from it, too, and my daughter, Marilyn, died from it in 1973. Arthritis had rusted out my hip joints to the point where I couldn't get around without a cane. In 1974 it confined me to bed, and I said that was it! My doctors had resisted performing surgery on me because of my diabetes and high blood pressure, but now I insisted on having one of those plastic hip joints even if it killed me. I'd rather be dead than forced to stay in bed. Well, it worked out fine. I threw my cane in the closet, and now my wife has to keep reminding me to slow down. Multiple sclerosis has handicapped my sister, Lorraine. She and her husband, Hank Groh, had three McDonald's in Lafayette, Indiana. My brother says Lorraine might have been a feminine Ray Kroc because she takes after me in many ways.

The foundation expanded its activities in 1976 to include a public awareness program relating to the effects of alcohol misuse on the family. The program is conducted under the name Operation CORK (Kroc spelled backward), and it is one of Joni's main concerns. She has devoted a lot of time and organizational effort to it, working with the Rev. John Keller and Fred Lane.

I have always enjoyed helping other people. It's the reason for my interest in the work of the foundation. It's also why, early in 1972, I decided I would celebrate my seventieth birthday that October by giving a significant amount of money to some worthy cause. A million dollars was the figure mentioned when I first discussed the idea with Joni and Don Lubin. It seemed like a nice, round number. But as the weeks and months went by and we drew up lists of possible recipients, the amount of money kept growing.

I planned to benefit Chicago institutions because Chicago is home for me and for McDonald's, and I wanted to show my gratitude. Another consideration was the fact that young people and families have been important to the success of McDonald's, and I wanted my gifts to acknowledge that. So my final list had major gifts to Children's Memorial Hospital, for genetic research and construction of new facilities; the Passavant Pavilion of Northwestern Memorial Hospital, for a research institute to study birth problems; Adler Planetarium, for the development of a Universe Theater; Lincoln Park Zoo, for construction of a Great Ape House; PACE Institute, for educational and rehabilitation programs for inmates of Cook County Jail; Ravinia Festival Association, to start an endowment fund; and Field Museum of Natural History, for a major exhibit on ecology.

It happened at the time these gifts were being considered that a blood donation day was organized at the McDonald's office in Oak Brook to help the young son of Red Llewellyn of our accounting department. The boy, one of ten children, was being treated for leukemia at St. Jude's Children's Research Hospital in Memphis, Tennessee, and he needed many blood transfusions. Red's wife came in later to thank me. She told me about what marvelous care her son had received at St. Jude's. So I did some investigating and learned more about the place. Then I added it to my birthday list.

In addition to the major recipients, I made contributions to Harvard Congregational Church in Oak Park, where I went as a boy, and to the Public Library in Rapid City, South Dakota, of which Joni was a trustee. When I added it all up, my birthday gift list totaled seven and a half million dollars. I'll tell you, it felt mighty good to be able to announce that kind of present!

As I said at the time, I had seen McDonald's become a national institution. America is the only country where it could happen, and I took genuine pleasure in sharing my good fortune with others.

My friends and business associates demonstrated in their birthday gift to me that they understood exactly how I felt. They established the Ray A. Kroc Environmental Fund at the Field Museum of Natural History. I was speechless with delight when it was announced by Leland Webber, director of the museum, that the fund had received more than $125,000 to provide educational programs such as film series, field trips, and workshops for young people.

To cap the celebration of my three-score-and-ten years, Joni threw a wonderful party for me in the Guildhall of the Ambassador West Hotel in Chicago. I was looking forward to seeing the faces of my closest friends, including many McDonald's employees—secretaries, field personnel, executives—that night, because I wanted to see their reaction to my birthday cards. They were in the form of gifts of McDonald's stock I had arranged for them to receive in the mail that day. In some cases the stock was divided between a man and wife and their children. It took a lot of undercover work to come up with all the social security numbers of spouses and children that were necessary to convey the stock and still keep the plan secret. But we managed it, and the surprise helped lift the spirit of the party to cloud level. I was particularly pleased to make the stock gifts to the wives of some of our executives, not only because they'd become my friends but because a McDonald's wife has to be a very patient and understanding person. I know that all of them make great sacrifices to allow their husbands to succeed, and I wanted to be sure that these women knew my concern and appreciation.

Talking about gifts and my philanthropies reminds me of one of the high points in my life. I have received a lot of awards over the years. My office in Oak Brook is a showcase for all these plaques and ribbons and trophies. Some people think it's kind of corny for the chairman of a large corporation to display such an array of mementos. But I'm proud of each one, from the rough, handmade tribute from a Boy Scout Troop to a goldplated Multimixer. But none of these awards gave me a bigger thrill than to be honored as *Ray A. Kroc, Philanthropist, Outstanding Chicagoan of Today* at a banquet given in 1975 by the Chicago Chapter of the National Multiple Sclerosis Society. With Joni's approval, I put my money where my mouth was in acknowledging the honor with a gift of a million dollars to the organization.

One thing I flatly refuse to give money to is the support of any college. I've been wooed by some of the finest universities in the land, but I tell them they will not get a cent from me unless they put in a trade school. Our colleges are crowded with young people who are learning a lot about liberal arts and little about earning a living. There are too many baccalaureates and too few butchers. Educators get long faces when I talk like this and accuse me of being anti-intellectual. That's not quite right. I'm anti-phony-intellectual, and that's what too many of them are. I'm definitely not anti-education. But my philosophy about what education should be is best expressed right in McDonald's own Hamburger U. and Hamburger High. Career education, that's what this country needs. Many young people emerge from college unprepared to hold down a steady job or to cook or do house-work, and it makes them depressed. No wonder! They should train for a career, learn how to support themselves and how to enjoy work first. Then if they have a thirst for advanced learning, they can go to night school.

We have thousands of success stories in McDonald's that followed exactly that pattern. There have been lots of unusual approaches, too. Take those nine sailors who came down from Great Lakes to see me about getting a McDonald's franchise in 1959. They formed a company called Careers, Inc., in Portland, Oregon. Careers, Inc., now has five McDonald's restaurants and is building a sixth. Ollie Lund has left Careers, Inc., and now has two McDonald's of his own. One of the original nine is dead, but the rest have prospered from their association with McDonald's. "I guess," Ollie Lund says, "McDonald's has been the making of all of us."

When I said thousands of success stories, I meant that literally. I couldn't begin to recount them. Some, like Lee Dunham, a former New York City policeman, have received a lot of public attention. *Time* magazine did an article on Lee and how he fought to keep his store open in Harlem. Other publications covered him, too. But the great majority of our winners are known only within the company, and they're all heroes to me—guys like Frank Behan, our Eastern zone manager, who had to be both father and mother to his children while struggling to get his store going. He did everything himself—his total mainte-nance bill the first winter was $4. These men and women join McDonald's from just about every conceivable calling. We've had college professors become operators, like Ed Traisman, who taught at the University of Wisconsin; Don Smith of Cleveland had been a judge; John Sirockman of Atlanta was a banker; Joe Katz of Detroit had been a practicing rabbi before he joined us;

Eli Shupack of Chicago was a CPA; John Kornblith of New York City was in the men's clothing business; and Dr. R. C. Valluzo of Baton Rouge, Louisiana was a dentist. We have several former military leaders like Colonel Marion MacGruder of Phoenix, Arizona, and professional athletes such as Jumping Johnny Green and Wayne Embry the basketball stars, and former pro football players Brad Hubbard of Atlanta, Tommy Watkins of Detroit, and Ben Wilson of Houston. McDonald's is a real melting pot.

The key element in these individual success stories and of McDonald's itself, is not knack or education, it's determination. This is expressed very well in my favorite homily:

"Press On: Nothing in the world can take the place of persistence. Talent will not; nothing is more common than unsuccessful men with talent. Genius will not; unrewarded genius is almost a proverb. Education will not; the world is full of educated derelicts. Persistence and determination alone are omnipotent."

That's the spirit that built 4,000 McDonald's hamburger restaurants. We dedicated number 4,000 in Montreal in September 1976, and it was a stirring experience. The celebration was tinged with sadness by the death of the husband of one of our stalwart operators. As if in keeping with that mood, the weather turned gray and rainy on the day of the ribbon-cutting ceremony. Nostalgia was keen among a theater full of top McDonald's operators and key corporation executives that morning. We saw a slide show that recapitulated our company's history in terms of past advertising campaigns and TV commercials. What memories! I felt for an instant as if I were back grinding it out, building the business all over again.

Then we went to the new store, which is across the street from the Montreal Forum. It's a beautiful building, this number 4,000. Strictly a city location—no parking lot—but the seating is on three levels, plus an open patio, and the modern lines with huge round windows in the mellow brick walls are just gorgeous.

The really breathtaking thing here, however, is the way the kitchen runs. It's like watching one of those movies where they speed up the film to make people move in a blurring rush. Of course, folks in that store have had plenty of practice in handling monster crowds. The unit opened during the Canadian Olympic games and did a phenomenal business during that trial-run period. In one week it grossed $74,000! By contrast, our first store grossed $6,969 in its first two weeks.

As George Cohon, President of McDonald's of Canada Limited, and Fred Turner and I got ready to cut the ribbon with 4,000 printed on it in great big numbers, the rain stopped. Maybe it was a good omen for the store. At least it pleased the newspaper and television cameramen. I told one of them, "We do it all for you."

Dedicating that restaurant was quite a milestone for those of us who could remember when we had four stores and were working like galley slaves to get number five. Now we're shooting for 5,000, and our confidence is so high that we even took a vote in Montreal to decide where number 5,000 will be built. Japan won. Personally, I'm thinking about number 10,000. A lot of people would say I'm dreaming. Well, they'd be right. I've been dreaming all my life, and I'm sure as hell not going to stop now.

I'm dreaming of a World Series title for the Padres.

I'm dreaming about new things for McDonald's International operations. Steve Barnes, who has directed our growth overseas, keeps coming up with exciting plans, and people everywhere— from Japan to Sweden—are welcoming the Golden Arches. Americans will be hearing a lot more about our hamburger diplomacy.

I'm also dreaming of some terrific new plans for McDonald's. My wife thinks I should take more time off and just sit in the sun; yet she knows I can't do that. I still work for the company every day at the jobs I know and like best—developing new menu items and new real estate projects.

In October 1976 I hired Renée Arend, former chef at the Whitehall, to be Executive Chef of McDonald's. His job is to study ways to make our menu more nutritious, get more fiber into it, and so forth, and also to help me refine recipes for new menu items.

Renée is a Luxembourger and his skill in the kitchen is the result of rigorous European training and lifelong dedication. He's concentrating all his talent on our simple menu, and the results will be culinary art in fast-food form. There are lots of things Renée and I will be working on. For openers, a new item I have in mind to help build our supper-hour trade. Renée is testing it, and if it turns out to be as good as I think it is, it will make the Colonel himself forget about fried chicken.

Our menu development, aimed at filling out a three-meal day plus snacks for our restaurants, has a parallel in our real estate planning. I mentioned the "nook and cranny" notion of real estate development and that's a good way of thinking of it. But the philosophy behind it is that we want to bring our restaurants to the people. We want to be where people live, where they work, and where they play.

Urban real estate is a different ball game than the one we play in suburbia where McDonald's grew up. This is especially true in commercial districts where people work. There, traffic patterns and eating habits create some unusual opportunities. For example, we can create vertical "rub-off" stores. Take Sears Tower in Chicago, one of the tallest buildings in the world; we could have put three McDonald's there, one in the basement, one midway, and one on the upper floors. All three would have done well, with the trade from one rubbing-off to the others and not encroaching at all. We didn't do that for various reasons, but we might try it somewhere in the future.

I was delighted when we made the decision that we would begin developing in downtown Chicago; it was a return to the old stomping grounds for me. I know every worthwhile location in the city, the delivery routes to it, and the kind of pedestrian traffic it gets. I also usually know who has the lease and for how long. What the hell, as I told Jack O'Leary, our district manager for the area, you can't peddle paper cups and Multimixers in a town for thirty-five years without learning something about it. And if you're sincere about serving your customer better, you learn the layout of his basement, what kind of alley access he has, and so forth. You might be able to suggest a better way for him to handle his stock or deliveries. That's what I always did, and now it's paying off for me in detailed knowledge that helps McDonald's. If you have this kind of attitude toward your work, life can't get you down, and that applies whether you are chairman of the board or chief dishwasher. You have to learn to know the joy of "working and being let work."

Too many young Americans these days don't get a chance to

learn how to enjoy work. Much of this country's social and political philosophy seems aimed at removing the risks from life one by one. As I told a group of business students in one of the talks I gave at Dartmouth, it is impossible to grant someone happiness. The best you can do, as the Declaration of Independence put it, is to give him the freedom to *pursue* happiness. Happiness is not a tangible thing, it's a byproduct—a byproduct of achievement.

Achievement must be made against the possibility of failure, against the risk of defeat. It is no achievement to walk a tightrope laid flat on the floor. Where there is no risk, there can be no pride in achievement and, consequently, no happiness. The only way we can advance is by going forward, individually and collectively, in the spirit of the pioneer. We must take the risks involved in our free enterprise system. This is the only way in the world to economic freedom. There is no other way.

Afterword

As I finish writing this book on December 31, 1976, I am painfully aware of the names I have not mentioned in it. Men like Reub Taylor, Commander Alexander B. Dusenbury, Ben Lopaty, Carl Reed, and a great many others who contributed significantly to the making of McDonald's. I can only ask all those who have been omitted to forgive me.

At this point McDonald's has 4,177 stores in the United States and 21 other countries. In the year just ended we broke through several boundaries to new levels of business activity and profitability. In 1976, for the first time, our total system-wide sales exceeded $3 billion: the revenue of McDonald's Corporation exceeded $1 billion. Our net earnings after taxes were more than $100 million, and our net worth was $500 million. The company is still green and growing, and so am I. As I look forward to my 75th birthday, everything seems to be coming up roses. I'll be able to tell you more *mañana . . . mañana . . .*

Ray A. Kroc
La Jolla, California

Index